LF 1 NORTH SEA ROUTE

Cycling between Den Helder and
Boulogne-sur-Mer

$s u s t r a n s$

P A T H S   F O R   P E O P L E

Fourth, revised and extended edition 1995

Stichting Landelijk Fietsplatform
Westvlaamse Vereniging voor de Vrije Tijd
Département du Nord
Translation, Sustrans 1996
Published by Sustrans 1996

The North Sea Cycle Route: a fine example

In the years since the war, attitudes towards the bicycle and cycling have diverged enormously between the UK and the Netherlands. While Britain and Ireland have neglected cycling, even discouraged it, the Dutch have put cycle routes, cycle parking, 'bikes on trains' and all the ancillary works that encourage people to cycle at the very centre of transport policy. It is this, combined with the easy terrain, which explains why the Dutch make almost 30% of their journeys by bike and we, a meagre 3%, although many parts of Britain have very similar topography.

The Noordzeeroute is an excellent example of modern cross-border cooperation, between local government (Conseil Général du Nord, France) a non-governmental body (Westvlaamse Vereniging de Vrije Tijd, Belgium) and cycle advocates (Stichting Landelijk Fietsplatform, Netherlands). Heavily used, and hugely beneficial to the local community, the LF1 route is only one of a network of national cycle routes crisscrossing the Netherlands and continuing over the borders into other countries.

This Dutch national network, and those in other European countries, have served as inspiration for Sustrans' National Cycle Network project. Our 6,500-mile Network will pass through every major town and city in Great Britain and Northern Ireland. It will run within a 10 minutes bike ride of 20 million people and is designed to demonstrate how quick, efficient and above all enjoyable cycling can be, when conditions are safe and attractive.

Sustrans' own target, for 20% of all journeys in the UK to be made by bicycle, may seem an ambitious one; it goes one step further than the Royal Commission on Environmental Pollution, which called for a quadrupling of cycling over the next 10 years. Yet the first sections of the National Cycle Network already attract enough new cyclists to suggest that the benefits of this project in utility cycling and in the tourism industry, as well as in reducing pollution and improving public health, may be enormous. The greatest challenge is to demonstrate to the general public and to policy makers that the bicycle is a transport of the future, so that the National Network comes to be a catalyst for cycling practice throughout the country

This guide, to a 470 km, largely traffic-free route in countries where the bicycle is a normal and respected way of travelling, will help many Britons to discover the full potential of cycling and to encourage their support for our National Network. I hope that planners and politicians will be prominent among them. Now it is clearly understood and accepted that the bicycle is a healthy and environmentally benign form of transport, we in the UK must bend our efforts to outdo the Dutch; to provide cycle routes and facilities which can be the envy of Europe.

John Grimshaw, Director, Sustrans

Foreword

The North Sea coast of Belgium and the Netherlands has long been an important holiday attraction. The variety of sea, dunes, scenic areas, characteristic towns and seaside resorts makes it a very attractive area. In 1989 the national cycle route that runs through this area was the first in the Netherlands to be signposted. LF 1, the North Sea Route, originally ran from Den Helder to the Franco-Belgian border opening up the most beautiful parts of the area to the holiday cyclist.

In 1995 a new step forward was made when the route was extended to Boulogne-sur Mer, bringing the total length to 470 kilometres. In France the route goes through a hilly area some distance from the coast and terminates at the well known white cliffs of the Boulogne-sur-Mer area. Through this extension a new element was added to the North Sea Route which has added great value.

Further extensions of the North Sea Route down the Atlantic coast and across the channel to the UK are envisaged. At its far end, in the North of the Netherlands, it connects to the LF 10 route through the Frisian Islands to the Dutch/German border.

The North Sea Route is the result of cooperation between the Département du Nord of France, the Westvlaamse Vereniging voor de Vrije Tijd (West Flanders Leisure Association) of Belgium and the Stichting Landelijk Fietsplatform (national cycling organisation) of the Netherlands. Project execution and maintenance is financially supported by the Province of West Flanders, the European Regional Development Fund (ERDF) and the Commissariat-General for Tourism (Belgium), the Dutch Ministry of Agriculture and Fisheries and the Provinces of North and South Holland and Zeeland as well as through cooperation with the French Département du Nord and the Fédération Française du Cyclotourisme.

Furthermore, the European Union has made this fully revised and extended guide possible through financial support from the Interreg programme between the North of France and Flanders.

Today, this route is a popular and well-known part of the network of recreational cycle routes in the Netherlands, Belgium and France. The route is ideal for cycle touring or day trips in combination with the use of public transport.

We wish the users of this guide very enjoyable use of the LF1 North Sea Route.

Amersfoort/Beernem/Lille
July 1995

Jacques Donnay MEP, Chairman Conseil Général du Nord
Jan Durnez, Executive Member West Flanders, Chairman WVT
Joop Borgman drs. Chairman Stichting Landelijk Fietsplatform

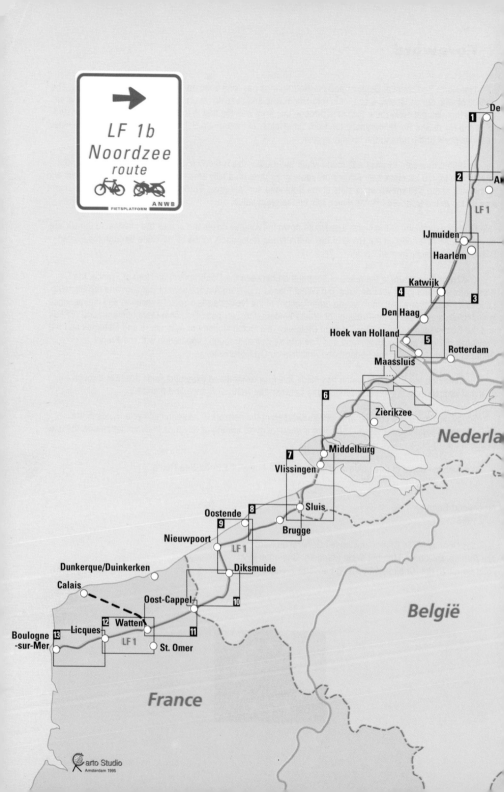

Contents

1. Introduction 6

2. The dunes of Holland and Flanders 10

3. The delta of South Holland and Zeeland 17

4. The Flemish polderland 20

5. French inland Flanders, Artois and the Boulonnais 23

Stage   1: Den Helder - Camperduin (32 km) 26

Stage   2: Camperduin - Noordzeekanaal (38 km) 30

Stage   3: Noordzeekanaal - Katwijk (37 km) 34

Stage   4: Katwijk - Hook of Holland (34 km) 38

Stage   5: Hook of Holland - Brouwersdam (56 km) 42

Stage   6: Brouwersdam - Middelburg (43 km) 46

Stage   7: Middelburg - Sluis (30 km) 50

Stage   8: Sluis - Oudenburg (36 km) 54

Stage   9: Oudenburg - Diksmuide (34 km) 58

Stage 10: Diksmuide - Oost-Cappel (28 km) 62

Stage 11: Oost-Cappel - Watten (37 km) 66

Stage 12: Watten - Licques (26 km) 70

Stage 13: Licques - Boulogne-sur-Mer (34 km) 74

Additional route: Watten - Calais 78

UK National Cycle Network for 2005 .... inner back cover

1. Introduction

In 1989 the first signposted Dutch national cycle route was inaugurated. The 370 kilometre long route ran from the ferry port of Den Helder to the Franco-Belgian border. In 1995 the route was extended to Boulogne-sur-Mer increasing its length to 470 kilometres. The route mainly uses traffic free cycle paths and quiet back roads through very attractive countryside and connects a number of interesting towns in the coastal area and its hinterland.

The route

Between Den Helder and Hook of Holland the North Sea Route follows the coastline, mainly through the dunes. The geographical conditions in the southern part of the Netherlands force the route to abandon the coastline more often.
The Belgian part of the route is situated much more inland than in the Netherlands, along the medieval tide-mark. You will cycle on dykes and on tow paths along the rivers and canals of the Flemish polderland, and enjoy the old scenery of inland Flanders near Bruges.

The French section avoids the busy towns of Dunkerque and Calais. The route runs some way from the coast, from east to west, through "Houtland", the hills of Artois and the Boulonnais. At Boulogne-sur-Mer you reach the distinctive white cliffs of the Channel coast.

The Dutch part of the North Sea Route forms part of the LF route network designed by the Dutch National Cycling Organisation (Stichting Landelijk Fietsplatform). The West Flanders Leisure Association (Westvlaamse Vereniging voor de Vrije Tijd) initiated the design of the Belgian section

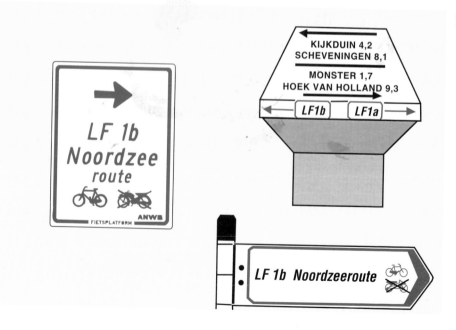

6   ▲ LF route signs

which also forms part of an LF route network developed by the Flemish Commissariat General for Tourism. In France, the FFCT and the Département du Nord initiated the design of the extension to Boulogne-sur-Mer, where the North Sea route is now the first signposted continuous cycle route.

Signposting

Signposting on the Dutch section of the route has been integrated where possible with the existing signing methods. Where integration is not possible and throughout the Belgian and French sections standard rectangular signs are used. All LF signs have a distinctive green italic inscription (see opposite).

Between the Franco-Belgian border and Watten (Ouatte) in France the standard LF signs are used Between Watten and Boulogne-sur-Mer a provisional method has been used which is expected to be replaced by standard signs as described above.

On occasion the signposted route may differ from that indicated on the maps in this guide. You should follow the signposted route.

The route guide

This guide is for the use of cyclists who do not wish to use the route as a means of getting to France or, in the opposite direction, to the island of Texel, as quickly as possible but for those who want to feast their eyes and dismount occasionally to enjoy towns and scenery more thoroughly.

Chapters 2 to 5 provide information about the dunes, the delta of South Holland and Zealand, the Flemish polderland and the French areas of inland Flanders, the Artois and the Boulonnais. Next, the numbered stages of the route are discussed including descriptions of interesting sites on or along the route. The stages are introduced by a map showing the route, accommodation, railway stations with a cycle hire facility and other features. Each stage is concluded by a selection of accommodation, museums and attractions and tourist information on or along the route.

In cases where international telephone numbers are indicated only the national numbers are provided. The prefix for Belgium is 00-32 and the initial 0 in the area code should be omitted. The international prefix for France is 00-33 and for the Netherlands 00-31.

The numbered stages are described in a north-south order. It is of course possible to follow the route in a south-north manner, using the guide in reverse order. This is facilitated by the division of the guide into stages and, within the stage descriptions, into different subjects introduced by **bold** headwords.

Accommodation

Each stage concludes with an accommodation list. The list is numbered, referring to the symbols on the map.

NJHC-hostels, despite their former name of youth hostels, are open to people of all ages. NJHC-hostels have separate double rooms as well as dormitories.
Information: 020-5513155 (The Netherlands) or 03-2327218 (Belgium).

All campsites listed accommodate cyclists. Campsites of 40 pitches or less are indicated as **small campsite** . These campsites are quiet and generally have limited facilities.
Country campsites are also small and quiet, with simple facilities. Often, they are situated in nature resorts and a countryside camping card is needed, which is available at ANWB offices. The country campsites are indicated with a special symbol ( ) For further information: Stichting voor Natuurkampeerterreinen (Association of Country Campsites), tel: Neth 0412-453713 (Tue-Fri from 10 am to 12 noon).
Some campsites have one or more **hikers huts**, small, simply equipped wooden homes for four suitable for cooking and sleeping. Campsite facilities can also be used. Campsites accommodating hikers huts are indicated by the hikers huts logo ( ).
Information: Stichting Trekkershutten Nederland (Dutch Hikers Huts association, tel: 026-3332033; Belgium: TFPA Tourisme Kempen (SPTA), Grote Markt 44, 2300 Turnhout, tel: 014-436111.

Farmsites, not included in the lists, are associated in two organizations.
The **Stichting Vrije Recreatie** (Association for Free Recreation) has over 1200 addresses of

proprietors, mostly farmers, who have equipped part of their property as a mini-campsite. For further information: SVR, Broekseweg 75-77, 4231 VD meerkerk (NL), tel: 0183-352741.
The second organization is the **Vereniging van kampeerboeren** (association of campsite farmers). A guide with over 500 addresses in the Netherlands can be obtained for ƒ 2,-. For further information: VeKaBo, Ettenlandseweg 25, 8316 RM Marknesse, tel: 0527-243339 (weekdays 1.30-4.30 am).

The **Hotels and Bed & Breakfast** addresses are only a selection of affordable accommodation offering secure bicycle parking. The prices mentioned are minimum prices for a double room with breakfast in 1995.
In **France** this heading also includes several **gîtes**, countryside houses which are rented to tourists, as well as a number of **chambres d'hôtes**, rooms with private house owners. For information and reservations in the Département du Nord: Informations touristiques sur le Département du Nord, Centrale de réservation, 15/17 rue du Nouveau Siècle, 59027 Lille Cedex, tel: 20570061.
In the Département du Pas de Calais: Réservations Loisirs-Acceuil Pas de Calais, 24 rue Désille, 62200 Boulogne-sur-Mer, tel: 21839677/21833259.
Lastly, for both departments: Comité Régional de Tourisme, Promotion touristique de la Région Nord/Pas de Calais, 26 place Rihour, 59800 Lille, tel: 20606962.

Not listed are the numerous addresses in the private sector, collected by the **Stichting Vrienden op de Fiets** (Accociation of cycling friends) which offer bed & breakfast for ƒ 20 - ƒ 25,-. A membership card and a booklet containing over· 1100 addresses can be obtained from the organization's secretariat for ƒ11,-: Brahmstraat 19, 6904 DA Zevenaar, tel: 0316-524448.

For **Belgium** a number of **holiday farms** are mentioned. These are bed and breakfast accommodation, some of which are no longer working farms.

Information on other possibilities can be obtained from VVV-offices (Netherlands), Tourism services (Belgium) and information points (France). Telephone numbers are provided at the end of each section.

Bikes and trains

It is of course not necessary to cycle the whole route; it can be split into several one-day trips, using the train. Dutch railways allow you to take a bicycle on the train for ƒ10,- single fare (journeys above 80 km ƒ15,-) or ƒ17.50 return (journeys above 80 km ƒ25,-). Generally it is not necessary to book but it is wise to check availability, especially when travelling in groups.
It is also possible to hire bicycles at the following NS and NMBS stations:

Den Helder	0223-619227
Castricum	0251-654035
Beverwijk	0251-226773
Haarlem	023-5317066
The Hague CS	070-3853235
Maassluis	010-5916988
Middelburg	0118-612178
Vlissingen	0118-465951
Brugge	050-385871 ext. 118
Ieper	057-201970

In the Netherlands, rental is ƒ 8,- per day, ƒ6,- for train travellers. Identification is required and a ƒ50,- (ƒ100,- in the Randstad area) deposit is payable by cash or cheque. In Belgium, rental is 250 bef. per day, 150 bef. for train travellers. An additional 100 bef. allows you to return the bicycle at a different hire point than where it was collected.

Payment of 500 bef. allows you to return the bicycle at a train station with no hire facility. The 500 bef. deposit will in this case not be returned. For British travellers, the chance to use a really cycle-friendly rail service is a delightful revelation. Take it if you can!

Comments about the route

Any remarks concerning the route, the guide or the signing can be addressed to:
For the Netherlands:
Stichting Landelijk Fietsplatform
Postbus 846
3800 AV Amersfoort
tel: 033-4653656
Complaints about the signing can be directly addressed to:
ANWB (Dutch National Tourist Bureau)
Postbus 93200
2509 BA Den Haag (The Hague)
tel: 070-3146786

For Belgium:
Westvlaamse Vereniging voor de Vrije Tijd
Kasteel Bulskampveld
8730 Beernem
tel: 050-781189
or **Provincie West-Vlaanderen** (Province of West Flanders)
Provinciale Technische Dienst der Wegen
Koning Leopold III-laan 41
8200 Sint-Andries Brugge
tel: 050-403367
or **Westtoerisme**
Kasteel Tillegem
8200 St.-Michiels Brugge
tel: 050-380296

For France:
Fédération Française du Cyclotourisme (FFCT)
52, rue du Marais
62220 Carvin
tel: 21406958
or **Conseil Général du Nord**
Direction de l'Environnement
Hôtel des Services
51, rue Gustave Delory
59047 Lille Cedex
tel: 20635745/20635959

For the United Kingdom
Sustrans
35 King Street
Bristol BS1 4DZ
Tel: 0117 926 8893
Fax: 0117 926 4173

2. The dunes of Holland and Flanders

The dunes and the polders beyond are specific to the Dutch and Belgian coast. This type of coast is relatively rare. The Atlantic coastline of Western Europe is over 15,000 kilometres long, only 3,000 kilometres of which consists of dunes; Almost 300 kilometres of these dunes can be found along the Belgian and Dutch coast. Other large dune areas are in Denmark, Germany and Northern France.

Dunes are characterized by an enormous natural diversity. The existence of many micro-environments in a line of dunes is the reason for this diversity: high, dry dune tips as opposed to low, wet valleys or hollows, windswept places and others in the lee, salty air close to the sea and less salty further away, sunny or shady places and many other combinations. In any of these micro-environments different plants and animals are at home.

The dunes cover just over one percent of the Netherlands. Nevertheless, 850 of the 1400 large plant species can be found here and 140 of 190 bird species breed in the dunes. The same applies for other plants and animals, such as moss, lichen, butterflies or beetles: the dune area is one of the richest ecosystems in the Netherlands. The Dutch dune area is particularly interesting since it is a long, continuous area which is relatively unspoilt.

The Belgian coastline is shorter than the Dutch, while the demand for seaside recreation is more or less equal. The Belgian coastal area is therefore very busy and large parts of the dune area have been developed. For this reason and because the Belgian section of the cycle route runs more inland this chapter highlights the Dutch dunes.

The history of the coast

In the eyes of geologists, who count in millions rather than in thousands of years, the Dutch coast is still very young. Wind, sun and sea are still forming the coast, although man has restrained their influence to a certain extent.

Approximately 20,000 years ago, during the latest ice age, the North Sea was largely dry. Much water was retained in the ice caps, which almost reached the Netherlands. After the ice age, melting ice raised the sea water level. Approximately 7,500 years ago the sea was still several kilometres off the current coastline. From east to west the coastal area consisted of a swampy peat area, a "wadden" area of clay sediment and a dune ridge closing the area off from the sea. This ridge consisted of material brought down by the rivers which was then moved by the sea and the wind.

As the sea level continued to rise more and more small dunes were formed and later destroyed, until - approximately 5000 years ago - the coastline reached its most eastern point. This is where the first dune ridge system was formed, the remains of which still exist: the dune ridge on which Rijswijk, Voorburg and Leidschendam were built.

After this period the sea level rose at a much slower pace. In addition, the rise of the sea level was more than compensated by the build-up of sediment. In other words, the sea was pushing itself back westward. The ridges that were formed in this process remained. Between the various dune ridges a freshwater environment developed and peat started developing. The dune ridges themselves became dunes due to a constant accretion of sand, which was consolidated by plants colonising the dunes.

This process of development of the old dunes continued until after the Roman empire.

During the middle ages the coastline started moving eastward again. Changing tidal movement and storm floods caused the coast to erode. The sea slowly moved inland via river mouths and tidal inlets. Near the village of Petten the coast broke, forming the tidal inlet of "het Zijpe". This inlet gradually extended north, east and south through the small river known as "de Rekere". Tidal trenches cut up the area into islands. The Belgian coastline was broken up by the same process near Nieuwpoort and Knokke. Here, a landscape of mud-flats developed, cut through by a network of creeks and ditches. These lands were gradually reclaimed through impoldering and drainage.

During this period young dunes began to be formed from the sand brought in by the eastward moving sea. At first these young dunes were only small sandhills on the beach. Later they became "mobile dunes" and moved eastward across the old dunes, driven by a strong west wind. These strong winds together with extreme drought kept the dunes from stabilising in one place. The strong wind also caused so-called "blow-outs" in the old dunes, sand being blown away as far down as ground water level, at which the wind could not move the wet and heavy sand grains. This process created ponds and wetland areas which exist to this day. Continuous accretion of sand also caused the mobile dunes to reach considerable height, as can still be seen near Bergen, Schoorl and Bloemendaal. Eventually, the mobile dunes were stopped by the woods in the east, some of which were planted by man as an emergency measure. This stabilizing work was accidentally undone by the introduction of the rabbit.

Rabbits in the dunes

The Dutch dunes were not the rabbit's original habitat. During the course of the 13th century, while young dunes were still being formed, the rabbit was imported from Spain as a hunting quarry and introduced into the dunes. Since then, one might say that the young dunes and the rabbit developed side-by-side. The nobility, owning the hunting rights in the dunes, leased them to professional hunters known as "duinmeiers" who hunted the rabbits for their fur. The rent that they received was their sole income from the dunes. Therefore, no means were spared to create as favourable an environment as possible for the rabbits. The "duinmeiers" had to feed them during the winter and natural ennemies were fought. Poachers risked having their eyes gouged out; farmers were only allowed to protect their land from rabbits by putting up fences and hedges; killing game was forbidden; dogs had one leg amputated which prevented them from chasing rabbits and cats had their ears cut off so that they could not go near the burrows without getting sand in their ears - a surprisingly effective deterrent. These kinds of rules were in force from 1300 until 1795 when the nobility lost its privileges.

The rabbit's rapid reproduction meant that they quickly came to dominate the ecology of the dunes, keeping down growth and maintaining them as an open and lightly vegetated area. Generally rabbits feed with low vegetation but when the low plants are covered with snow in the winter they eat bark from trees and shrubs, which subsequently die after some time. Also, tree felling and grazing cattle have contributed to the development of the dunes in this way although the influence of the rabbit has been predominant. It can be concluded that the rabbit has assured the great natural diversity of the dunes today and still prevents them from growing thick with coarse vegetation such as thorns and reeds. This makes the little animal very popular with conservationists, in the dune area if not everywhere

else in Europe.

Protecting the dunes

In the latter half of the 19th century new measures were introduced to counteract the shifting sands caused by grazing, treefelling and the aforementioned rabbits. As an experiment, pine trees were planted at numerous places along the coast. Those planted too close to the sea were badly affected by the salty air and by the rabbits. It was not until the end of the century that woods were planted on a significant scale. The black pine was particularly popular with foresters because of its straight grain and suitability for woodwork. It also grows extremely well in the dunes and can still be found in the area around Schoorl. Black pine woods are not particularly attractive because of the dense, regimented planting which hardly allows any other vegetation to grow except fungi. Nowadays different kinds of pines as well as deciduous trees are

▲ **Rabbit in the dunes**
photo: WVT

planted and more room is left open between them, which makes for a much more varied landscape. The pine woods are also made more attractive by careful and imaginative forestry; when trees are felled, others which are older and taller are left to give character to the woods. We find these woods mostly on the western side of the dunes where they are not affected by the heavy sea winds. Nevertheless, the wind is heavy enough to "shave" the edges of the woods.

The part of the dunes closest to the sea serves above all as a sea defence, which prevents the west of the country from being flooded. At the same time this strip of dunes is the most vulnerable, because it is the part where the wind is fiercest and vegetation most scarce. It also has to stand up to the power of the waves. Protection from the wind was achieved by planting marram grass and by placing rows of tree branches in the sand. This kind of protection however created a very artificial landscape (a straight sand dyke) with low scenic value. Perpendicular breakwaters were built to reduce the impact of the waves, and nowadays dune erosion is counteracted by spraying new sand on the beach,

which is cheap and creates a more natural effect. The sand sprayed onto the beach breaks the power of the waves, although it may itself be partly washed away. Sometimes new small dunes are formed with this "artificially" added sand.

In the future, new methods will be needed to protect the low-lying parts of the Netherlands from the rise in sea level forecast as a result of global warming. This threat may help to explain just why the Netherlands is so forward-thinking in terms of transport, and in particular of cycling infrastructure.

Agriculture

Since the Middle Ages most of the old dunes have been converted into farmland. Woods were cleared and dunes were levelled so that the groundwater was closer to the crops. Initially the ground was used for all kinds of agriculture since there was no other cultivated farmland available in the west of the country. From the 17th century, as the polders developed, agriculture and cattle breeding could slowly be moved to more suitable ground. The so-called "ghostgrounds" - sandy soil between the dunes and the polders - could now be used for market gardening which became more and more important with the growth of the cities. Later the lucrative bulb-growing industry developed, for which a sandy and level ground is very suitable.

The Sea village landscape

The first people in the west of the Netherlands settled in the dunes, the hinterland being unsuitable. Until about the year 1000, people mainly lived in the eastern part of the dunes, making their living by agriculture and fisheries. In the period that followed, which coincided with the formation of the young dunes, people started moving westward and fishing villages emerged which we now know as the seaside resorts of Egmond aan Zee (developed from 970), Zandvoort (1120) and Wijk aan Zee (before 1300).

Coastal erosion was caused by the rise in the sea level and the many storms, exacerbated by the damage to dune vegetation as a result of grazing and tree-felling, and this was the reason why many villages were moved. Much of the farmland was covered with sand and in the "haaygemeten", which still exist near Ouddorp on the island of Goeree, the sand was removed from the farmland and used to build walls serving as protection from the wind. In

12   ▲ **Black (left) and coarse pine**

other areas, people took to fishery, to profit from their proximity to the sea. Since they used flat-bottomed vessels which were pulled into the sea from the shore, no ports were dug.

Until the late Middle Ages the fishing villages were rather prosperous. There followed a period of great difficulty caused by many storm floods. This period ended in the latter half of the 19th century and tourism started to take over from fishery as the dominant economic sector. Even today though, statues of women, sometimes with children, stare out towards the horizon, recalling the fate of the many fishermen who never returned from sea.

Until the 19th century agriculture was impossible in the young dunes. Cultivation of the land had always been encouraged but the few attempts undertaken failed within several years due to soil depletion and flooding. In spring and autumn the cultivated valleys were mostly inundated. In the latter half of the 19th century potato culture developed on a small scale, stimulated by high prices after the potato disease of 1845. Depletion of the soil made it necessary to cultivate new land every two to three years. Also, the land had to be dug lower in order to get closer to the ground water level, which began to fall as a result of water extraction. The material which was dug up was used to build small dykes which protected the fields from the wind and at the same time served as field boundaries.

Since the beginning of the 20th century fishery has been concentrated in harbour towns such as Den Helder, IJmuiden, Katwijk and Scheveningen, due to the growing use of large vessels. Tourism income reduced the need to rely on the potato crop, further threatened by blight and a drop in the groundwater level caused by water extraction. During World War II potato culture in the dunes revived somewhat but after the war most of the land was abandoned. Some stretches are now being used as allotment gardens such as can be found around Zandvoort, Wijk aan Zee, Castricum and especially Egmond aan Zee. This remarkable mixture of agriculture, other human activities, dunes and transitional areas around villages is called the "Sea village landscape". These landscapes are attractive not only from a scenic point of view but also attract unique flowers and birds. The importance of the remaining sea villages has now been widely recognised and they will in the future be protected from the growth of towns and villages.

Country estates

The inland dunes have always been very popular, at first because of a lack of alternative settlement lands, later because of the attractiveness of the area. In the 17th and 18th century nobility and rich people from the cities built beautiful country estates with extensive parks, which served as summer homes. The dunes were a perfect hunting area. Until the 18th century the gardens of these country estates were in a geometric French design, followed by an era where the English country style was extremely popular with meandering paths, streams and hills suggesting a charming, natural scenery. Most of the country estates which still exist are built in this style. Collossal trees grow along the lanes, mainly beeches and oaks, and the ground is grown with the so-called stinzenflora (e.g. wild hyacinth, snowdrop, anemone), most of which escaped from cultivation.

Water extraction

Today the dunes are of great importance for water extraction. In 1851 the city of Amsterdam started extracting water from the dunes after pollution of its existing water supply had caused a cholera epidemic. This example was followed by many other towns when the cholera epidemic of 1866 appeared to ignore Amsterdam and instead hit 17% of the people who still obtained their drinking water from a pump or well.
Water extraction is harmless to the dunes as long as rainfall exceeds the quantity extracted. However, when houses were connected to a mains water supply system, causing water consumption to rise dramatically, the water level in the dunes started falling quickly. Dune lakes ran dry and the unique flora disappeared. At this point water had to be extracted at a greater depth from a freshwater reservoir which fills up only very slowly. This method is still used among other places in the Kennemer dunes.
In 1940 Leiden became the first city to filter water from the Rhine through the dunes. In the 1950's this method began to be adopted on a large scale. Pre-purified river water is carried by canal to the dunes where it is run into and filtered by the sand, before being pumped up. After final purification the water is ready for consumption. This purification process naturally pollutes the dunes somewhat which can cause rare plants like orchids to disappear in favour of nettles.

In order to prevent this from happening a new extraction method is now proposed: **depth infiltration.** Water is pumped into wells at a depth of 50 to 70 metres and pumped up again from another well at the same depth. This method does not disturb the dune surface and it also allows water to be purified outside the dune area. It is also slightly more expensive than traditional methods causing the price for the consumer to rise, but it is hoped that this will simply discourage people from wasting water.

On a small scale the depth infiltration method is already used in the North Holland Dune reserve near Castricum, the water supply dunes of Amsterdam and in Meijendel. It is planned to start a number of large projects in the dunes between Katwijk and The Hague. If this environmentally friendly method of water extraction catches on the valuable, wet dune valleys could be restored.

In the past years the water companies have made many efforts to improve their environmental image. Not only are they improving the purification process, they have also spent a great deal of money on improving the pre-purification of the infiltration water. They take better care of their operational environment and try to minimise damage to flora and fauna. Some companies have stopped water extraction in parts of the dune area altogether. The Amsterdam Water Company has recently closed a water extraction canal in their dunes and between Katwijk and The Hague the water company has decided to clean up areas of the dunes along the North Sea Route allowing the natural environment to be restored over the next few years.

However, the dunes are still drying out. Apart from water extraction, two other main activities account for this: neighbouring agriculture and foresting. Since man began extracting water from the dunes the water level has dropped by two to three metres, which has caused the loss of valuable flora and fauna.

Nature and recreation

The recreational importance of the dunes is very much based on their beauty and variation. Going inland from the sea in a straight line is a transect through history from young dunes and valleys to old, developed ones. The changing conditions are home to an equally changing population of plants and animals.

The **first embryo dunes** are created by the wind and as easily destroyed by a change in wind direction. If the wind does not change direction grass may grow stabilising the dune with its roots and allowing it to grow. This grass is strong enough to grow through a layer of sand that may be thrown onto it by the wind and can resist an occasional salt wave.

When the dune is approximately 1.5 metres high marram will start growing. Apart from marram there is very little vegetation and apart from seagulls very few birds.

We find these emerging dunes on the Wadden and in some parts of Zeeland where the dams built as part of the Delta Works have allowed new dunes to be formed. On the coast of Holland the situation is quite the opposite. There human efforts are constantly required to prevent the erosion of the dunes.

On the dunes further east we find a more miscellaneous vegetation with thorns and thistles, elder and privet. All these plants are fairly resistant to drought and the salty air on the high dunes close to the sea.

Here and there behind the dune ridge we can find the **primary dune valleys** in between the youngest and the second line of dunes. The vegetation is very varied because of the many transitions: between salt and fresh, between wet and less wet, between fertile and barren. Some rare plants can be found that do particularly wel in wet environments like the parnassia and the marchwespenorchis, an orchid that can be found on Voorne. The "Brede Water" (wide water) on Voorne is a good example of a primary dune valley.

Behind the primary dunevalleys we find the classic **open dunes** which have already been influenced by man, animals, wind and vegetation. The southern slopes have a low cover (e.g. moss, fern) because of their exposure to bright sunshine. The northern slopes are much greener, especially

▲ **Dune lake near Huisduinen**

during the summer, and are covered with shrubs such as privet and blackberries, and with herbs. Animal life is also rich and varied. This is very much the domain of the rabbit. They come out especially at dusk but their presence is made very clear during the day by their burrows and the pellets at their so-called latrines. Abandoned burrows are used by birds to nest in.

Stoats, polecats and foxes hunt for rabbits. During the Middle Ages foxes were wiped out by dunewardens but they reappeared in 1968 and their number is growing. Foxes are night animals and apart from rabbits eat birds, insects and fruit.

Next on our journey we pass through the **secondary dune valleys** with their distinctive ponds formed by wind erosion (the aforementioned "blow-outs"). Along the route they can be seen in the North Holland Dune Reserve and in the Kennemer Dunes. In and around the ponds live green and brown frogs, along with other water animals such as beetles, dragonflies and mosquitoes. On a warm summer evening you can enjoy the concert of the toads.

The next section of dunes is more protected from the wind and therefore covered with higher vegetation. The plants that grow here are elder, privet, thorns, spindle trees, roses and hawthorn. Hawthorn is not very resistant to the sea wind and so develops a typical bent and shaven form. These shrubs attract many insects which are food to the nesting birds: nightingales, sparrows and wrens. This scenery can particularly be found in Meijendel, north of The Hague.

The most inland part of the dunes is the **duneforest**, which will be passed en route between Beverwijk and Overveen. By now, the sea wind has lost most of its strength and the soil has been fertilised - by many generations of plants that have died and decayed - to the point that it can sustain trees. The most beautiful woods are the oak woods in the aforementioned country estates. In other parts, on the edges of the polders we also find woods of alder and birch. There are many insects and therefore many insectivorous birds such as woodpeckers and robins. On the edge of the woods and in the open fields we sometimes see roe deer. As a result of intensive hunting roe deer disappeared from the dune area for a long time. Hunting restrictions are allowing them to return to their habitat. Particularly in the dunes owned by the Amsterdam Water Company many roe deer can be

seen but in other parts of the dunes too they are gradually beginning to re-appear.

The vegetation in the dunes differs according to the degree of lime in the soil. The dunes north of Bergen and on the Wadden host different kinds of heather and broom which do not grow on a lime-rich soil. The southern dunes will possibly develop in the same way because of acid rain, which is neutralising the lime. Another threat is airborn nitrogen pollution. Nitrogen in the rain fertilises the soil which allows coarse grasses to take over.

Cyclists and walkers in particular are attracted by the beaty of the dunes and they enjoy this beauty to the full, in a way no motorist can. Some people merely want to take in the fresh air and enjoy the scenery, others stop to investigate every plant meticulously. It is good that the dunes have been opened up to the non-polluting traveller with walking and cycle paths, for this is a very benign kind of tourism, with minimal environmental impact. However, nature will suffer if people gather en masse or leave the paths. Vegetation can easily be damaged or even destroyed and shy or vulnerable animals will leave these areas. Therefore, please do think about the impact of your visit and try to minimise it, which you have already done, of course, by your choice of transport.

Young dunes ▶
photo: Guillaume Lemoine

Access for cars is restricted to a small number of roads which have been built in a straight line towards the beaches. On the one hand there are roads to the seaside resorts, on the other the "slagen", such as the Langevelder slag and the Wassenaarse slag, that lead to large car parks close to the beach. This is where beach visitors and walkers go their separate ways. The cyclist however, who rides along the whole coast, sticks to the cycle paths in the dunes and only has to cross occasional roads carrying motorised traffic.

3. The delta of South Holland and Zeeland

At the beginning of the Christian era the south-west coast of the Netherlands was unbroken. This situation changed drastically and permanently at the beginning of the Middle Ages due to numerous floods which swept away the dunes and the peat behind. The water that flooded inland divided the land into islands, many more than exist today and differently located.

Moving coastlines

The history of the Dutch coastal area has always been one of battles against the sea. In 1953 the biggest-ever flood took place in the South-West of the Netherlands. This led to the enormous undertaking of the Delta Works, to stabilise a coastline which until then had been constantly moving.

On the one hand, man annexed land that had run dry, on a large scale from the 12th century onwards. The numerous dykes show how the current coastline was formed and in how many stages. The more recent dykes are generally closer to the coast. An important part in the reclamation of land (impoldering) was played by the monasteries. Many Flemish monasteries were given extensive properties in Zeeland which they cultivated, of which the most important were the Cistercian abbeys of Ter Duinen and Ter Horst.

On the other hand enormous pieces of land had to be given back to the sea at times. On maps they are described as "drowned lands (verdronken land)". Between Yrseke and Bergen op Zoom, for example, lies the drowned land of the Markiezaat of Bergen op Zoom. These areas were flooded in 1530, including the then important city of Reimerswaal. At low tide parts of these areas run dry and old objects are sometimes found.

Better known is the drowned land of Saeftinge in the Western-scheldt north of Zeeland-Flanders. This area is mostly dry and has a vegetation of lavender and sea bead.

Inundations

Sometimes land was handed to the sea intentionally. This happened in wartime when the enemy was cut off using the water as a tool. During the Eighty Years' War the front line between the

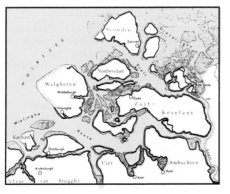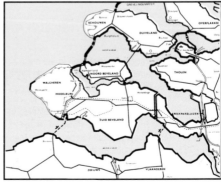

▲ Zeeland c. 1300 (left) and today

Spanish troops and those of the Prince of Orange moved continuously. This line was near the current Dutch-Belgian border. Because of the constant movement of the front line fortresses were built in different places, many of which still exist or are at least clearly recognisable. The coves that were formed in Zeeland-Flanders when the sea water could move back and forth freely still exist.

This so-called inundation method was used for the last time in 1944 by the Allied troups. In order to break the German resistance the Island of Walcheren was inundated by bombing the dyke in four different places: at Vlissingen, east of Rammekens, at Veere and Westkapelle. The coves, when the coast was closed again, developed into nature reserves.

Residential history

The earliest traces of occupation in the area were found in Haamstede and suggest people living here since 2100 BC.
Floods in the third century BC forced people to abandon the area until shortly after the beginning of the Christian era when the water slowly retreated. Numerous Roman objects from the period until the year 273 were found, such as the famous images of Nehellennia, Godess of the sea.

Later, another period of floods left the area abandoned. After the land ran dry again, villages were founded in the high parts of the area safe from the sea.

In the 19th Century the coast was threatened by attacks from the Vikings. As a defence, 'burgen' were built on the high ground. These buildings measured 150 to 200 metres in diameter. The "burgen" later developed into towns such as Middelburg, Domburg, Oost-Souburg and Oostburg. The burgen can still be identified at the very centre of the town maps of Middelburg and Oost-Souburg.

Before water defence works started there were hardly any residents in the rural areas. Some farmers lived on artificially constructed hills which were later developed in the so-called "vliedbergen", refuge hills. This name was given to them because they were originally thought to have served as a place of refuge from the rising water. Now it is believed that they had a military function. They were situated behind farms and were mostly occupied during times of threat of war. The island of Walcheren notably still has many "vliedbergen".

Until the 14th Century the towns of Aardenburg, Sint Anna ter Muiden and Sluis were extremely prosperous. These towns benefited from the important position of Bruges which from the North could only be reached by ship via the bay of the

"Zwin". After the Zwin silted up Antwerp took over Bruges' position and the aforementioned towns of Zeeland-Flanders collapsed. Towns situated at the Scheldt estuary now started benefiting from the pivotal position of Antwerp. Then, in 1585 during the Eighty Years' War, Antwerp was lost to the Spaniards and the regime of Holland blockaded the Scheldt. Towns in Holland and Zeeland took over Antwerp's trade and Middelburg became the second most important Dutch seaport behind Amsterdam. But by the end of the 18th Century Zeeland was no longer an important trade route and its period of prosperity ended. From then until the 20th Century Zeeland was a sparsely populated area where people mainly lived off the land.

After the Second World War a turnaround came with the growth of mass tourism. The coastal area enjoyed a growing popularity, and the Delta Works not only made the area safer but increased accessibility. The construction of a number of dams cut off the lake of Veere and the Grevelingen from the sea, offering great opportunities for the development of water recreation.

▲ **Dyke bordered with poplars**   ▲ **Small dyke on Voorne-Putten**   19

4. The Polder lanscape of the Belgian Coast

The Belgian polders have not long been in permanent cultivation. Former inhabitants often had to abandon the area when the sea level rose due to rising global temperatures which melted the polar ice caps. These periods, lasting several centuries, were followed by periods of falling temperatures during which the sea withdrew.

Floods in the Middle Ages

The Middle Ages were characterised by the so-called "Dunkirk transgression" phases, periods of severe flooding. Most notably the Dunkirk II transgression (c. 400 AD) changed the landscape radically. The sea washed away almost all the existing dunes and the water invaded the land by approximately 15 kilometres depositing clay on the original peat soil. During the eighth century the sea withdrew and new dunes were formed.

Shortly after the year 1000 the sea level rose again marking the beginning of the Dunkirk III transgression. These floods had less impact than those which came with the Dunkirk II transgression. During the Dunkirk III the Zwin between Cadzand and Knokke and the river IJzer estuary near Nieuwpoort were formed. The Zwin penetrated inland until it reached Bruges giving the town a direct connection with the sea. Along the Zwin many seaports developed such as Sint Anna ter Muiden, Sluis, Hoeke and Damme. The first primitive dykes kept the plains along the sea coves partially dry. The dykes were built from the 11th century perpendicular to the coast along both sides of the coves. The western side of the river IJzer was closed by the still existent Old Seadyke between East-Dunkirk and Lo, the eastern side was closed by the Zidelinge between Bredene and Oudenburg.

From the 13th century the sea withdrew reasonably quickly. Large parts of the flooded land ran dry and were colonised by man. New settlements, including Nieuwpoort, were built on the reclaimed land.
The sea withdrew more slowly from the Zwin and the IJzer. The abbeys played a considerable part in the impoldering of the IJzer while the impoldering of the Zwin was initiated largely by civil servants and nobles from Bruges. The Zwin was eventually reduced to nothing more than a small stream which finally silted up completely. The once blooming towns, cut off from their predominant source of activity, now went into decline.

Reversal of the contours

When the sea receded, the first inhabitants of

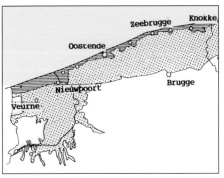

▲ Shoreline during Dunkirk II transgression

▲ Shoreline during Dunkirk IIIa transgression

the polders colonised the raised areas where clay had been deposited on top of the existing peat and had protected it from erosion. Over time, however, as the sea level fell the peat drained and lost volume, and was compressed by the weight of the clay. Meanwhile, the drainage channels, where sand had settled instead of clay, retained their original height, as the once - high ground sank past them. Thus, the relief map of the landscape was gradually reversed, to the point where the inhabitants, finding their settlements regularly flooded, had no option but to move uphill to the crests of what had once been drainage channels.

Nature and farming

Being situated only slightly above sea level and often even below, polders are extremely vulnerable and could easily flood if not protected by dykes. Agriculture is only possible when artificial means are used to keep the water out. Nevertheless, on the lower, wet terrains a varied habitat has a chance to develop. Life in the water (eg. fish and algae) or near the groundwater (eg. worms) is food for different kinds of birds. The varied topography of the area, high and low, wet and dry, contributes to a diverse and fascinating flora and fauna.

Unfortunately, modern farming is driven by imperatives hostile to a diverse natural environment. The ideal conditions for monoculture, such as artificial fertilisation, drive out some plants, while others are treated as weeds and eradicated. Mechanisation leads not only to flattening out of the landscape and removal of trees - to permit efficient machine working - but also to drainage aimed at creating a firmer surface for agricultural machines. The flora and fauna of the drained land change, eliminating the food supply for birds such as lapwings and black-tailed godwits.
Where farming, landscape and natural diversity used to go hand in hand they are now clearly incompatible. Places where these elements can still

▲ **The Zwin**
Photo: WVT

live together are becoming increasingly rare.

Fortunately, farming and nature are still able to co-exist reasonably well in the polders of West Flanders. Much pasture land along the route is extremely beautiful from a scenic point of view and is host to many birds. Many goose species for example winter in the area around Damme. The IJzerbroeken area, which is often flooded during the winter, is among the richest areas of Flanders in terms of bird population.

Trees are very scarce in the polders. They can mostly be found along the canals, for example the poplars along the Damse Vaart and the many different species of deciduous trees along the canal from Bruges to Ostend. People used to plant pollard trees and hedges as property boundaries but nowadays they can only be found on farmyards and along roads. They give both farmer and cyclist some protection against the sometimes fierce western winds and are host to many animals. The real treasure of the polders, however, are the many ditches, ponds and canals containing water plants such as fern and duckweed. The water is full of perch and water beetles.
It is fortunately true that large parts of the polders are not only farmland but at the same time provide valuable wildlife havens.

▲ **Camomile and cornflowers**   ▲ **Falcon**

5. French Inland Flanders, Artois and the Boulonnais

As we enter France we leave the flat landscape behind us: Between the border and Boulogne-sur-Mer we will climb 200 metres. The slopes of Inland Flanders are gentle, although the Wattenberg on the edge of this area is fairly steep (72 metres). From the Wattenberg the route goes downhill towards the valley of the river Aa before joining the hills of the Artois. Near Licques the route runs through a low-lying area, before a steep climb to Colembert at 200 metres where your efforts will be rewarded with a magnificent view of the Boulonnais. Through the flat land of the Boulonnais we head towards Boulogne-sur-Mer with its "Côte d'Opale" where we can admire the steep white cliffs.

The geology of this rolling landscape shows enormous variation. The layers that are found on the surface vary in age from the Primary to Quaternary period. Ground movements, fluctuation of the sea level and erosion have created a varied landscape where each place has its specific geological trademark. Flora and fauna as well as man have adapted themselves to these changing conditions.

French Inland Flanders

Although this area is still relatively flat it differs a great deal from the Flemish polderland. In Inland Flanders eroded material from higher areas surfaces a 150 metre thick layer of compact clay from the

Tertiary, approximately 70 million years old. Here and there streams cut through which feed the river Yser. In the Artois this layer of clay has eroded and in the Flemish coastal area the layer is covered by young sediments.

The soil is very fertile and suitable for growing a wide range of crops. Blue and white flowered flax is still grown here, as are the hops which have returned after a period of absence.

The farms, hamlets and villages are very dispersed partly because water was always widely available. The traditional farm is the U-shaped farmstead built around a courtyard, the entrance

▲ Regions of northern France

facing south. The farmsteads were generally built at the centre of the holding, which would be surrounded by a long hedge or a row of trees. The name of the area, **Houtland** (Woodland) derives from this traditional planting, although many hedges and trees have disappeared over the past few decades. Fortunately measures are now being taken to reverse this decline in tree cover. New hedges and trees are even being planted.

In this area we mostly find oak trees and even some oak woods, for example in Esquelbecq. The ash is the next most important tree since the elm was largely wiped out by elm disease. The hedges still consist for a large part of hawthorn despite the impact of disease.

Tourism is beginning to develop in this area, witness the growth in the number of farms or **gîtes** which offer accommodation to tourists. This form of low-impact tourism will undoubtedly develop further. The planned creation of an international nature reserve will contribute, as, we hope, will the growing cycle tourism on the North Sea Route.

The Flemish Mountains

South of the route we can see the gently rolling landscape with its rounded hills. The history of this landscape goes back many millions of years when the sea invaded the present Flanders and the north of France and deposited a thick layer of clay and sand.

This layer has disappeared in many places due to erosion, but not in this area where wide valleys were formed by the many streams and rivers. Erosion had least effect on soils where the surface material was transformed into sandstone. Thus, ranges of hills were formed separated from each other by the valleys of the streams and rivers. They are often called **Getuigenheuvels** (witness hills).

The ecological conditions are favourable for the development of beech woods, which require a

permeable soil. In the spring we also find large areas of bluebells. On the sometimes steep slopes the woods and scrub have been able to survive, the thin soil being insufficiently fertile for farming.

The area is rather sparsely populated. **Cassel** has remained the centre since Roman times. Just south of the village of Wylder, which lies along the route west of the bridge over the A25, runs the **Steene Straete**, a Roman road to Cassel.

The Audomarois

The Audomarois is a wet area between Flanders and the Artois in the valley of the river Aa. This swampy area is a Regional Park, the centre of which is **Romelaere**, eight kilometres south-east of Watten.

The Audomarois is a beautiful symbiosis between natural and human influences which came into being around 1000 years ago. The marshes or "marais" are crisscrossed by a network of ditches and canals, through picturesque nature areas and farmland. Traditional farming, "maraîchage", is still practised on these parcels. It is worth making the time to take a boat trip in the traditional vessels: the "bacôves".

The Artois

Approximately 50 million years ago geological movements lifted this area to a higher level than neighbouring Flanders. Erosion has had a notable effect on the transitional area between the two regions and on the brook valleys, bringing older, deeper layers to the surface. First, the **chalk** which was deposited some 100 million years ago by the "chalk sea". This layer was cut in the valleys of the rivers Hem, Aa and Lys, and others. Further west, in the Boulonnais, the youngest chalk layer has disappeared altogether in some places. The slopes being subject to erosion, loam and grit were deposited at the foot. This is clearly visible around the woods of Eperlecques.

The Artois is the highest area along the North Sea Route with its peak at 211 metres. On the plateau intensive farming is the main activity (grain and beet). The valleys on the other hand are predominantly green. The pattern of settlement is just as differentiated, with a small population concentrated into settlements on the plateaus, greater numbers more evenly spread in the valleys.

▲ **Wood with bluebells**

A highlight of this area is its contact with the sea, the steep white cliffs of **Cap Blanc-Nez**, 15 kilometres west of Calais, towering 134 metres above the waves. Immediately behind the coast we find extensive gently rolling meadows rich in orchids and other flora. The most important function of the regional park is to preserve the native vegetation through effective management.

The Boulonnais

This area is lower-lying than the Artois. The Boulonnais is extremely varied from a scenic point of view thanks to the three rivers that formed so much of its landscape: the Slack, the Wimereux and the Liane.
As mentioned above, the upper chalk layer has disappeared due to erosion allowing layers dating back 100 million years to come to the surface. The layers that were uncovered by the rivers, such as loam, sand, chalk, limestone and marble, as well as the contours make for a great diversity of vegetation.
The chalky soils are mainly overgrown with small plants, among which are many types of orchids. This vegetation survived thanks to intensive grazing by rabbits and sheep keeping the vegetation short and the ground arid. Later, many fields were abandoned and neglected. Plant matter was no longer removed, organic material accumulated making the soil more nutritious which caused less rare plants and shrubs to overgrow the ground. In the nature reserve this development is now being halted by introducing sheep and horses which keep the vegetation short. Farmers are rewarded for using their land extensively which encourages a more diverse vegetation.

The hedges typical to this area are well preserved: the hawthorns are trimmed well and a number of woods still survive, especially ash. There is also a multitude of orchards, where many people make their own cider. The houses with their white facades are spread over the entire area and are very much in harmony with the landscape.
The coast with its cliffs and dunes also has great scenic value. **Cap Griz Nez**, ten kilometres north of Boulogne-sur-Mer, is the most striking element of the Boulonnais coast although there are other similar places.
Geologists, botanists and ornithologists, and ordinary nature lovers too, will find this a fascinating area through which to cycle.

▲ **Mill on the Wattenberg**

SCALE 1: 150.000

5 km

Key

30	LF1 Route, distance to Den Helder (km)
	Other signposted LF routes
	Signposted ANWB cycle routes
↑ 24125	Numbered ANWB sign
	Cycle path
	Other path
	Train station with cycle hire
	Tourist Information (VVV)
	Ferry, pedestrian-only ferry
	Railway with station, museum railway
	Motorway, junction, with cycletrack
	Rural lane, private road
	Minor road
	Main road, main road with cycle ban
	Unmetalled road
	Dyke
	River, canal
	Viaduct, bridge or tunnel
1	NJHC hostel (Youth Hostel)
2 2	Hotel, NIVON house
3	Nature campsites
4	Other campsites
5	Hikers hut

} numbered in accommodation list

	Recreation area, swimming
	Animal park or deer park
	Nature reserve
	Cemetery
✈	Airport
	Factory
	Pumping station, dam or sluice
	Windmill, water mill
	Timber framework clock tower
	Castle, ruin
	Noteworthy building(s)

	Town or village
	Lake
	Wood or park
	Slope
	Heath
	Quarry
	Dunes
	Sea

Den Helder - Camperduin

The northernmost point of the route is at the terminal of the **ferry** between **Texel** and **Den Helder**. The town of Den Helder is surrounded on three sides by the sea. Major industries include the naval port, fishery, shipping and tourism via the ferry. Being a **naval port**, it has an important military function. Den Helder has been host to the navy since it moved here from Hellevoetssluis in the 17th century. The naval port is situated on the eastern side of the town behind the ferryport. Also important in the development of Den Helder was the **merchant navy**. Until 1876 ships from Amsterdam heading for the sea passed Den Helder, up to 1824 sailing through the Zuiderzee, then more frequently using the Noordzeekanaal. Either Oudeschild, a town on the eastern side of the island of Texel, or Den Helder were the door to the North Sea. Sailing ships could only make their passage if the wind was in the right quarter; sometimes the necessary weather conditions did not occur for weeks. While anchored at the "Rede van Texel" the sailors visited Den Helder for provisions and entertainment.

The end of the cold war and subsequent cuts in defence budget have big implications for the town of Den Helder. The navy has already, or will in the future, cut thousands of jobs. It is hoped to compensate by increasing tourism. In the grounds of **Fort Kijkduin** near Huisduinen, abandoned in 1989, guided tours are now organised and at the end of 1995 an **aquarium** was opened. The big attraction here is a 40 metre diameter tank where a glass tunnel gives the visitor a sense of actually being in the water. There are also 11 smaller aquaria.

The coast between Den Helder and Camperduin has a very narrow dune strip. About 1,000 years ago, near Huisduinen and Callantsoog where the dunes are wider, there were two islands: **Huisduinen and 't Oghe**, the result of a series of breaches in the dykes and the only remains of the formerly uninterrupted coastline. Between 1300 and 1500 the coast closed up again when the tidal inlets silted up. Few dunes were formed in this process, so sanddykes were built, which became the basis for the narrow dunestrip; apart from these sanddykes normal seadykes were also built.

The **seadykes** are situated between Den Helder and the small seaside resort of Huisduinen (with its 64 metre tall cast-iron lighthouse) and between Petten and Camperduin. The cycle route follows

both dykes, so you can enjoy the wide view over the sea without being disturbed by motorised traffic. The dyke between Petten and Camperduin is known as the **Hondsbosse Zeewering**, after the village of Hondsbos, devoured by the sea. It was first built in the beginning of the 17th century after the dunes were swept away. Because of the great danger of the sea invading again three dykes were originally built, called the guard, the sleeper and the dreamer. When the guard dyke was considered strong enough to withstand the sea alone the other two were removed. The position of the Hondsbosse Zeewering, a hundred metres further into the sea than the dunes north and south of it, shows how much land had been lost to the waves since 1823 when the dyke was built. After the Hondsbosse Zeewering was built the area west and north of Westfriesland was gradually impoldered. Just over one kilometre north of Camperduin is the little wildlife area of **De Putten**, formed from the borrow pits from which material was dug to build the dyke.

Between Huisduinen and Callantsoog, where the island of 't Oghe used to be, and between Callantsoog and Petten, **sanddykes** were built as a coastal defence. The first sanddyke was completed in 1610. As you cycle along the edge of the narrow

▲ **Lighthouse, Huisduinen** 27

prevent dirty water from the polder from running into the wildlife resort of Het Wildrijk. This also created favorable conditions for frogs and spawning fish.

Between Sint Maartenszee and Petten you will regain the edge of a narrow dune strip. The dyke which caused their formation was completed in 1572. This dyke closed off the Zijpe, a channel which connected the North Sea with the Wadden Sea and which formed a threat to West Friesland. It was therefore important for the whole of North Holland as far as Amsterdam to close off this channel and to impolder it. After the first difficult closure, the Zijperdijk broke three more times before becoming permanent in 1597. Later, the wind deposited sand on the dyke and it has now become part of the dune.

Just north of **Petten** are a striking variety of modern **windmills**. They are on the ECN (Energy Centre Netherlands) grounds and are used in wind energy experiments. On these grounds there is also a small nuclear plant which mainly operates for medical purposes. Among other things it is used for the production of isotopes for cancer diagnosis.

Here too is the **Wereldwindorgel** (world wind harp) which consists of 99 five metre bamboo pipes in three groups. The notches in the pipes give the wind a specific note which is louder as the wind blows harder.

dunestrip that developed around it, you have a good view of the polders, an important bulb growing area. Between Huisduinen and Callantsoog you pass the holiday villages of **De Zandloper** and **Groote Keten.**

Between Callantsoog and Sint Maartenszee you will find the wildlife resort of **Het Zwanenwater**, which can only be entered on foot. It contains two large dune lakes which were formed by the wind in the 18th century. This area has an extremely varied flora because of its poor soil and the many transitions from dry to humid. The soil is deliberately kept poor by mowing the plants once they have finished flowering, rather than let them die back into the soil.
The southern part of Het Zwanewater connects to the **Zuidduinen** (the South dunes), which are the remains of the dunes of the former island 't Oghe. These dunes are thus about a thousand years old and have reached an advanced stage of development.

North of Sint Maartenszee a **duinrel** - a small gully filled with seepage water from the dunes - runs alongside the road. In 1993 a dam was built to

▲ **Wind harp, Petten**

Accommodation

Hotels and guest houses
1- **Den Helder**, "Wapen van Den Helder", Spoorgracht 43-44, 0223-622240. ƒ 70,-
2- **Den Helder**, "Lands End", Havenplein 1, 0223-621570. ƒ131,50
3- **Den Helder**, "Golden Tulip Beatrix Hotel", Badhuisstraat 2-10, 0223-624000. ƒ185,-

Campsites
1- **Den Helder**, "De Donkere Duinen", J. Verfailleweg 616, 0223-614731
2- **Callantsoog**, "De Nollen", Westerweg 8, 0224-581281 ()
3- **Callantsoog**, "Klein Begin", Abbestederweg 11, 0224-581277
4- **St. Maartensvlotbrug**, "t Ruige Veld", Ruigeweg 49, 0224-561291 ( )
5- **Petten**, "Bremer", Westduinweg 180, 0226-381767 (small site)

Tourist attractions

Den Helder
Käthe Kruse doll museum
Binnenhaven 25, 0223-616704
Den Helders naval museum
Hoofdgracht 3, 0223-656902
Dorus Rijkers Museum of Maritime Rescue
Bernhardplein 10, 0223-618320
Roundtrips
on the Marsdiep, to Oudeschild (Texel) and Terschelling

Huisduinen
Fort Kijkduin (aquaria at disused fort), Admiraal Verhuellplein 1, 0223-612366*
De Lange Jaap (lighthouse), 0223-620509

Petten
De dijk te kijk (history of the Hondsbosse Zeewering, Zuiderhazedwarsdijk, 072-5193636*

Tourist information (VVV)

Den Helder, Bernhardplein 18, 0223-625544*
Callantsoog, Jewelweg 8, 0224-581541
Petten, Zijperweg 1A, 0226-381352

29

From Camperduin to the Hook of Holland, the Dutch coast is characterised by a continuous line of dunes, only interrupted by the Noordzeekanaal. Almost all the stage uses cycle paths straight through the dunes. Most of the dunes between Camperduin and the Noordzeekanaal form part of the Schoorl forest and the North Holland Dune Reserve. To enter the latter a ticket (f2,- 1995) is obtainable at the entrances: north at the VVV-office of Bergen aan Zee and south through a ticket machine at the Oudendijk north of Beverwijk.

The dunes are widest - a maximum of five kilometres - on the northern part of this section as far as Bergen. Here, they also attain their maximum height. The wooded dunes to the east reach a height of over 50 metres.
Until **Schoorl** you roughly follow the edge of the pine woods, planted since the end of the 19th century, with its attractive views of a dune lake and its
seagull colony. This colony, which settled on the dunes of Schoorl in the early 1960s, can be observed at close range from an **observation hut** near the route.
Where the route crosses the cycle path linking Schoorl to the beach is the **De Berekuil** visitor centre from whence guided tours through the dunes are organised. From here to Bergen aan Zee the route runs through the woods, which are only 600 metres from the sea - as close as the sea winds and salt air will permit trees to prosper.

Bergen aan Zee was founded at the beginning of the century as a coastal resort to the town of Bergen. In the centre of the village are exclusive residential areas. Originally, these contained spacious Springer houses alongside the much more austere designs typical of the architect Berlage. The small peace church with its thatched roof was built after the First World War. Many of the original buildings were destroyed during the Second World War.
The Van der Wijckplein features a **Sculpture** representing a woman with a fish, by the artist Nic Jonk who died in 1994. Observant cyclists will discover more of his work along the route.

The dunes between Bergen and Egmond aan Zee have an extremely varied flora, the soil varying from lime-rich to acid. Many kinds of orchids grow here.
Around **Egmond aan Zee** we find the purest example of a landscape on which the old seaside villages were built. Typical features are the small hollows excavated in the dunes where the combined influences of man and nature have created a remarkable vegetation. Some of these areas were "handed back" to the dunes, other are still used for small-scale market gardening. The part directly north of Egmond is part of the **Wimmenumer Duinen**, also called **Six's dunes** after their former owner. As there is no cycle path built here yet, for three kilometres the route follows an old road along the edge of the dunes, where you will pass the beautiful residential area of
Het Woud.
The town of **Egmond aan den Hoef** developed around a 12th century castle, founded by the Heren van Egmond (the Lords of Egmond). The castle was destroyed by fire in 1574 but the foundations and the moats are still intact. These remains, together with the Reformed church and its surrouding area including farmlands have been a protected area since 1970.

Het Woud ▶

You can reach the Wimmenumer Duinen via the Nightingale path on the northern side of the village. Your ticket to the North Holland Dune Reserve is also valid here.

Just south of the road from **Castricum** to the seaside you will see the site where the North Holland provincial water company infiltrates river water into the dunes for purification. A little further south is a glider airfield.

South of the North Holland Dune Reserve the route goes through the **market gardens** on the "geestgronden" - the sandy soil between the dunes and the polder - near Beverwijk. This region is famous for its strawberries.
Meanwhile, if you have cycled from north to south you will have seen the impressive chimneys of the **Hoogovens plant** approaching. This collosal steel plant was established in 1918 because of its proximity to the sea for the supply of metal ore. Gradually, the Hoogovens have taken over enormous parts of the dune area between Wijk aan Zee and Beverwijk. Sadly, the plant pollutes the area heavily with metal-based emissions.
Between Beverwijk and the Hoogovens the route passes a number of fortifications which were built in 1799, during the French era, as part of the **line of Beverwijk**. Other sides of the town were defended through a system of fortresses and floodable fields. The line of Beverwijk was too high above sea level to be flooded and therefore ramps (earth defence works) were built.

The route goes along the edge of Beverwijk,

partly on the small road called **"Holland op z'n smalst"** (Holland at its narrowest). The name recalls the time when the Zuiderzee reached as far as the old dunes near Velsen. Holland was thus kept together by this small strip of land where Holland was therefore narrowest. In 1863 a breach was made in Holland op z'n Smalst to give Amsterdam direct access to the sea. The Noordhollands Kanaal, used since 1824 was no longer sufficient, not only because of the detour but also because the meandering channel became more and more tricky for ships of increasing draught and because Amsterdam feared competition from the port of Den Helder. English engineers were brought in for their technical expertise and the sand dug away from the dunes was used to build two parallel dams through Het IJ (the IJ lake) and the Wijkermeer. In between these dams the **Noordzeekanaal** was formed. The land alongside was impoldered. You could almost say that the construction of the Noordzeekanaal involved no more than leaving a trench while reclaiming the Wijkermeer and Het IJ. However problems such as strikes and financial difficulties delayed construction of the section through the dunes, the mouth of the canal and the piers. The canal was not inaugurated until 1876.

Accommodation

Hotels and guest houses
4- **Schoorl**, "Strandhotel Camperduin", Heereweg 395, 072-5091436, ƒ120,-
5- **Bergen aan Zee**, "Hotel Meijer", Jac. Kalffweg 4, 072-5812488, ƒ140,-
6- **Wijk aan Zee**, "Hotel De Klughte", Van Ogtropweg 2, 0251-374304, ƒ120,-
7- **Wijk aan Zee**, "De Wijck", Van Ogtropweg 12, 0251-374350, ƒ105,-
8- **Wijk aan Zee**, "Mare Sanat", Rijkert Aertszweg 8, 0251-374364, ƒ80,-

NJHC hostels
1- **Egmond**, "Klein Rinnegom", Herenweg 118, 072-502269
2- **Bakkum**, "Koningsbosch", Heereweg 84, 0251-652226
3- **Heemskerk**, "Slot Assumburg", Tolweg 9, 0251-232288

Nivon houses
1- **Bergen aan Zee**, "Het Zeehuis", Verspijckweg 5, 072-5813090, inf.: 072-58121971
2- **Wijk aan Zee**, "Banjaert", Burg. Rothestraat 53a, 0251-374318, inf.: 020-6941449

Campsites
6- **Schoorl**, "Koningshof", Duinweg 99, 072-5091510 (🏕)
7- **Schoorl**, "Buitenduin", Molenweg 15, 072-5091820
8- **Egmond a/d Hoef**, "De Woud-hoeve", Zandweg 30, 072-5061744 (🏕)
9- **Egmond aan Zee**, "De Egmonden", Nollenweg 1, 072-5061702
10- **Limmen**, "Limmen", Hogeweg next to no. 181 (🏕)

Tourist attractions

Bergen aan Zee
Aquarium (fish and shellfish), V.d. Wijckplein 16, 072-5812928

Bergen
't Sterkenhuis (history of Bergen), Oude Prinsweg 21, 072-5897028/5894116
Kranenburgh Museum (Bergen art in 1882 mansion), Hoflaan 26, 072-5898927

Castricum
De Hoep Visitor Centre (flora and fauna of the dune reserve), Johannisweg 2, 0251-6662235

Egmond aan Zee
Egmond Museum (history of Egmond), Zuiderstraat 7, 072-5063233/5061678
Prins Hendrik Foundation Museum (model ships), Voorstraat 41, 072-5061224

Egmond aan de Hoef
Castle chapel, Slotweg, 072-5064605/5062033 (appointment necessary)

Egmond-Binnen
Egmond Abbey Museum (excavations), Abdijlaan 26, 072-5061415

Tourist Information (VVV)

Groet, Heereweg 210, 072,5091423
Schoorl, Duinvoetweg 1, 072-5091504
Bergen aan Zee, Van der Wijckplein 8, 072-5812400
Egmond aan Zee, Voorstraat 82a, 072-5061362
Beverwijk/Wijk aan Zee, Julianaplein 3, 0251-374253

◀ In the dunes of Schoorl

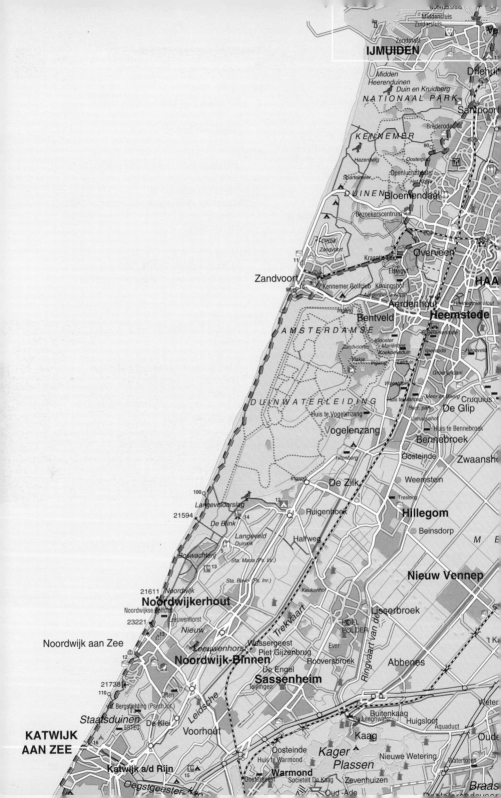

You will cross the Noordzeekanaal by ferry where a rail bridge used to be until in 1959 it was replaced by a rail tunnel. As an alternative, two kilometres to the west you can cycle across the top of the sluices. Looking towards the sea you can see a **fortified island** which, during the Second World War, was part of the German Atlantic Wall, although it was not an island then. In 1884 a smaller version of the fort already existed, as an outpost of Amsterdam. Later, it became an island because of the widening of the Noordzeekanaal.

The town of **IJmuiden** developed after the opening of the Noordzeekanaal, much against the will of Amsterdam which was still afraid of competition from rival ports. A major factor in its development were the fishermen who in rough weather sought refuge between the piers and at the mouth of the channel. Later, a fish market was set up here. The fishing port of IJmuiden was given an extra boost when the Zuiderzee was closed off from the sea in the mid 1930s. Many sea fisherman moved here from Urk, among other ports. IJmuiden is predominantly an industrial town, however, due to the influence of the Hoogovens steelworks mentioned in Stage 2.
The former centre of the town was demolished by the Germans during World War Two to give a clear field of fire. Other parts of the town were destroyed by bombing.

East of IJmuiden the route continues along the grounds of the Velserbeek estate and passes two other country estates; Beeckestein and Waterland. The latter is still privately owned. These are among many country estates which were built on the west bank of the Wijkermeer, mainly around Velsen and Beverwijk, between the end of the 16th until the mid 18th century. These often served as summer homes to aristocrats from Amsterdam. The area was popular because of its accessibility - only a few hours by boat - and its hunting.
Velserbeek was originally built in the 17th century, but the existing white house dates from the 18th century. The park was then transformed to the fashionable English country style with hills, ponds, little islands and meandering paths. Although the whole estate was landscaped, it still suggests a natural countryside. The ponds are situated around the Engelmandusbeek, one of the few remaining streams that rise in the dunes. **Beeckestein** still has the very rare, original 17th century geometric garden design which never ran wild. The house has a museum with 18th century style chambers and the Felix Tal fan collection. In the park we find two winding "snake walls".

Near Velserbeek a cycle tunnel leads under the road to what is left of **Velsen Zuid**. The village is stuck in between this provincial road, the Noordzeekanaal and the road towards the Velsertunnel. In the course of the century almost

half of the village has been sacrificed to the widening of the Noordzeekanaal; in 1906, 1939 and 1969. The oldest part was preserved and has been a protected village since 1970. It is mainly composed of 18th and 19th century houses, but the **Engelmunduskerk** is the oldest church in the area and was founded shortly after the year 700 by Willibrordus and named after a preacher who spoke here in the eighth century. The oldest remaining parts of the church date from the 11th century.

The oldest road in this area is the **Driehuizerkerkweg**, which you will ride on from Velsen Zuid south across the country estates. The road was constructed in the ninth century on the former inner dunes.

Near Santpoort you will join the road that follows the current dunes. Slightly further north you will see **Duin en Kruidberg**, a huge neo-renaissance country estate from the early 20th century which is now used as a conference centre by the ABN-Amro bank. On this spot, 300 years ago, stood the manor where William III lived before his marriage to Mary. Around the estate is a park and a wildlife resort. Your ticket for the Kennemerdunes (see below) is also valid here.

One kilometre to the south is the **ruin of Brederode**. The castle was built in the 13th century. After the Spaniards had destroyed it in 1573 during the siege of Haarlem it was abandoned and gradually deteriorated.

A little further and you ride through the **Kennemerduinen** National Park (tickets obtainable at the entrance; ƒ1,75 in 1995) with its rich vegetation typical to calcareous soils. South of the Kennemerdunes you will again find yourself among the country estates which were built in this area in every form. You will also pass the back of the **Elswout** estate. This was built in the mid 17th century and contains, apart from the house, a beautiful orangery. The garden, which was originally in a geometric French style, was transformed into an English style in the 18th century. It has several giant trees and exotic flora. For a small charge you can walk in the garden.

This is also the place where the road crossed a canalised **duinrel**, a small stream that rises in the dunes, which connects to the Brouwersvaart in Haarlem. This stream once supplied the Haarlem breweries along the river Spaarne with water.

From Kraantje Lek you will return to cycle paths through the dunes. **Kraantje Lek** is a 40 year old watering hole where fishermen on the way to Haarlem with their catch used to stop to quench their thirst. The path leading from here to Haarlem is therefore called the **Visserspad** (fisherman's path). The original 17th century path was replaced by a railway in 1881. The contemporary path of the same name runs parallel to the railway and was built in 1979.

The town of **Zandvoort**, like the seaside resorts further south towards Scheveningen, has developed from a fishing village to a buzzing seaside resort. The great attractions apart from the beach are the casino and the racing circuit.

South of Zandvoort a cycle path along the sea will lead you along the **Amsterdamse Waterleidingduinen** (dunes of the Amsterdam Water Company) where water from the Rhine is purified for drinking water.
You will continue through the dunes, but it may be pleasant in spring to ride to the edge of the dunes near Noordwijkerhout and enjoy the view of the **Bulb fields** on the "geestgronden" between the dunes and the towns of Lisse and Hillegom.

Further south again you will follow the boulevard of **Noordwijk** whith a view of the sea. Noordwijk is an ultra-modern seaside resort. However, Queen Astrid Boulevard still exudes the bygone atmosphere of the resort.

▲ **Orangerie, Elswout**

Accommodation

Hotels and guest houses

9- **Zandvoort**, "Faber", Kostverlorenstraat 15,
023-5712825,
ƒ110,-
10- **Zantvoort**, "Bad Zandvoort",
Thorbeckestraat 23, 023-5713520,
ƒ100,-
11- **Zandvoort**, "Zuiderbad", Boulevard Paulus
Loot 5, 023-5712613,
ƒ145,-
12- **Noordwijk**, "Sonnevanck" Koningin
Astridboulevard 50, 071-3612359,
ƒ110,-
13- **Noordwijk**, "Panorama", Oude Zeeweg 74,
071-3612920, ƒ130,-

NJHC hostels

4- **Haarlem**, "Jan Gijzen", Jan Gijzenpad 3,
023-5373793
5- **Noordwijk**, "De Duinark", Langevelderlaan
45, 0252-372920

Campings

11- **Driehuis**, "Schoonenberg",
Driehuizerkerkweg 15a, 0255-530144
(▲)
12- **Ruigenhoek (Noordwijkerhout)**, "Ruigenhoek", Vogelaarsdreef 31, 0252-375002 (▲)
13- **Noordwijk**, "De Carlton", Kraaiers-
laan 13, 0252-372783 (🚐)
14- **Noordwijk**, "Jan de Wit", Kapelle-
boslaan 10, 0252-372485 (🚐)
15- **Rijnsburg**, "Koningshof", Elsgees-
terweg 8, 071-4026051 (🚐)

Tourist attractions

IJmuiden

Pieter Vermeulenmuseum (natural science),
Moerbergplantsoen 20,
0255-536726

Velsen

Beeckestein (country house, fan collection),
Rijksweg 136,
0255-512091

Santpoort

Ruin of Brederode (mediaeval implements),
Velserenderlaan 2,
023-53787763

Zandvoort

Cultural centre
Gasthuisplein 9b,
023-5761570

Lisse

Keukenhof (flower exhibition),
Stationsweg 166a,
0252-419034
Bulb fields museum, Heereweg 219,
0252-417900

Noordwijk

Noordwijk Space Expo
Keplerlaan 3, 071-3646446

Tourist Information (VVV)

IJmuiden, Marktplein 42, 0255-515611
Haarlem, Stationsplein 1, 023-5319059
Zandvoort, Schoolplein 1, 023-5717947
Noordwijk, De Grent 8, 071-3619321

In its early days, **Katwijk** was a typical fishing village but now it is primarily a seaside resort. During the Second World War most of its buildings were demolished when the coast was cleared to deter Allied landings. Before the war the village had many characteristic white houses. Almost all of these have disappeared, except for the 17th century house on Louwestraat, which is still in almost perfect condition. Most buildings along the boulevard were built shortly after the war. The simplicity of the building style of post-war Katwijk is in sharp contrast with that of the nearby modern town of Noordwijk. One of the reasons for this is that the Reformed Church feared that allowing Katwijk to become too fancy a tourist attraction would endanger Sunday churchgoing.

Katwijk is the town where we find the mouth of the **Old Rhine**. A memorial stone next to the sluice commemorates the joining of the Rhine with the North Sea in 1807. An earlier attempt in 1572 failed because the canal was much too narrow and silted up almost immediately.

The most important buildings of Katwijk along the route are the **Oude Kerk** (old church) which dates from 1709, the **Vuurbaak** from 1605 which, after the Brandaris on Terschelling, is the second oldest lighthouse in the Netherlands, and the **Soefi-tempel** (1990) built in the dunes.

The route from Katwijk to The Hague passes through open dunes with many ponds of various sizes. The water from these ponds is filtered to supply drinking water to the towns of Leiden and The Hague. East of the cycle path south of the Wassenaarse Slag, in the area where water is purified for The Hague, are the **Meijendel** woods, containing a visitor centre. From 1830 this area was used as farmland but due to disappointing revenues the landowner decided around 1916 to sell the land as building plots for villas. The municipality of The Hague feared that their water extraction activities would be threatened by this plan and decided to purchase the land compulsorily. The water company then planted these woods, mainly consisting of trees and shrubs native to the dunes.

The route goes through the conurbation of The Hague via the green belt between The Hague and Scheveningen which is mainly dominated by country estates or their remains.

During the latter quarter of the 19th century **Scheveningen** had already developed from fishing village to a seaside resort of international reputation. The **Kurhaus**, completed in 1885, was the focal point of numerous villas, hotels and leisure centres. Later, the boulevard suffered from a period of decline, until after 1970 a major renovation programme was begun. Many of the late 19th century - early 20th century buildings were replaced by new hotels, appartment blocks, shops and other modern facilities. The Kurhaus only just survived this face-lift; it was converted and thoroughly renovated, but is now surrounded by new buildings. The **pier** is another landmark, which is now owned by the Van der Valk corporation and is being extended with a restaurant and halls. Nevertheless, fisheries are still an important activity for Scheveningen. In 1973 a new fishing port, with a fish market, was inaugurated.

The Hague is the seat of the Dutch Government. The first buildings of this town were built in the 13th century on the very spot where the Government still sits: on the Binnenhof. The counts of Holland founded a castle at the centre of their hunting areas: the "haag" to which the settlement owes its name. Het Haagse Bos, where Queen Beatrix occupies the Huis ten Bosch, is one of the remnants of this estate.

The Hague was able, until the industrial revolution, to expand its territory substantially, because the town was never given "stadsrechten" - city rights -

▲ **Soefi temple, Katwijk** 39

which would have obliged it to build a city wall. In other towns all the buildings had to be built within the city walls, creating a dense, urban style of development but the nobility of The Hague had space to build large estates with gardens and parks right in the centre of the town.

The cycle route runs alongside parks that were of later development. From north to south you first pass the **Nieuwe Scheveningse Bosjes** (new woods of Scheveningen) along the Pompstationweg. These woods were first planted in the 1930s by unemployed people on work programmes. During the Second World War the trees were felled by the Germans and set in the ground as pointed stakes to deter allied parachutists. After the war the area was built up with domestic waste from The Hague and trees were replanted.
At the end of the Wagenaarweg you see the **Westbroekpark**, developed in the 1920s. The hills were created after the war when the German bunkers were covered. The centrepiece of the park is a flower garden with a particularly beautiful rose garden.
On the other side of the canal you cycle through the **Scheveningse Bosjes** which contains the miniature town of **Madurodam**. Eastwards, across the Teldersweg you pass a playground named **De Bataaf** after an exiled Batavian who in 1798, with government support, tried to cultivate an area of dunes. The attempt naturally failed.

In the **Van Stolkpark**, an exlusive residential area developed from 1873, is the junction with route **LF4, the Midden -Nederland route** which runs from here to Enschede in the east of the Netherlands. A guide to this route is available from Stichting Landelijk Fietsplatform (p.9) but only in Dutch. You now cross the oldest metalled road in the Netherlands, designed by Constantijn Huijgens and completed in 1665. Detouring eastwards on this road for a short distance, you find the **Zorgvliet** estate on your right. The estate was developed from 1652 by the then 75 year-old poet "father" Jacobs Cats. This house is now the residence of the Prime Minister of the Netherlands.

Via the port of Scheveningen and the working-class quarter of Duindorp you again reach the dunes. First, you pass the **Westduinpark**. At the beginning of the 20th century the dunes were so heavily exploited that the vegetation disappeared and the dune began to erode. In 1925 the area was therefore closed apart from the paths, fertilised with domestic waste and replanted.

South of The Hague the dunes gradually become narrower and lower. Between Ter Heijde and the Hook of Holland the route follows a cycle path on the edge of area called the Westland, **"De glazen stad"** (the glass town) which occupies a large part of the rectangle bounded by The Hague, Delft, Vlaardingen and Hook of Holland. The "geestgronden" are covered with greenhouses where vegetables, fruit and cut flowers are grown.

▲ **Beach-bar, Scheveningen**

Accommodation

Hotels and guest houses
14- **Katwijk**, "Pension Seagull", Noordzeepassage 62, 071-4014436, ƒ60,-
15- **The Hague/Scheveningen**, "Seabreeze", Gevers Deynootweg 23, 070-3524145, ƒ100,-

NJHC hostels
6- **The Hague**, "Ockenburg", Monsterseweg 4, 070-970011

Nivon house
3- **Hook of Holland**, "A. Reitsmahuis", Nieuwlandsedijk 160, 0174-382560, Inf: 0181-614931

Campsites
16- **Katwijk**, "De Noordduinen", Campingweg 1, 071-4025295
17- **'s-Gravezande**, "Jagtveld", Nieuwlandsedijk 41, 0174-413479*
18- **Hook of Holland**, Wierstraat 100, 0174-382550   (🅿️)

Tourist attractions

Katwijk
Katwijks Museum (history of Katwijk), Voorstraat 46, 071-4013047
Round trips on the lakes of Holland province

The Hague
Haags Gemeentemuseum (post 1800 art and implements), Stadhouderslaan 41, 070-3381111
Haags Historisch Museum Korte Vijverberg 7, 070-3646940
Letterkundig Museum (Literary museum), Prinses Irenepad 10, 070-3471114
Mauritshuis (14th and 17th century painting), Korte Vijverberg 8, 070-3654779
Rijksmuseum de Gevangenpoort (Instruments of punishment and torture), Buitenhof 33, 070-3460861
Rijksmuseum H.W. Mesdag Laan van Meerdervoort 71, 070-3635450
Museon (popular science), Stadhouderlaan 41, 070-3381338

Panorama Mesdag (large realistic panorama painting A.D. 1881), Zeestraat 65b, 070-3642563/3106665
Omniversum (space film theatre), Pres. Kennedylaan 5, 070-3545454
Madurodam (miniature town), Haringkade 175, 070-3553900

Scheveningen
Schevenings Museum (fisheries and archeology), Neptunesstraat 92, 070-3500830
Zeebiologisch Museum (marine biology), Dr. Lelykade 39, 070-3502528
Round trips along the North Sea coast
Sealifecentre (aquaria), Strandweg 13, 070-3542100

Tourist Information (VVV)

Katwijk, Vuurbaaklaan 11, 071-4075444
Noordwijk, De Grent 8, 071-3619321
The Hague, Koningin Julianaplein 30, 06-34035051 (50 cts/min)
Scheveningen, Gev. Deynootweg 126, 06-34035051 (50 cts/min)

41

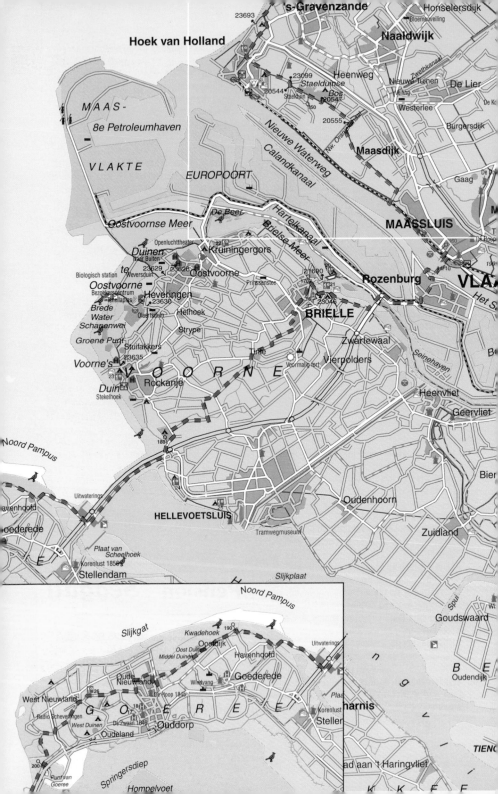

Since 1872 the coastline near Hook of Holland has been broken by the **Nieuwe Waterweg** (new waterway) which gives Rotterdam a better connection to the sea. Until the beginning of the 18th century this connection was the tidal inlet of Brielle but when it silted up the route could no longer be used. For a long time Rotterdam could only be reached through long detours e.g. via Dordrecht. The Waterweg is an inlet open to the sea like the Western Scheldt. In order to comply with the safety requirements of the Delta Plan the river dykes in the area around Rotterdam and Dordrecht had to be raised, but further risk assessment showed that the dykes were still too low. This problem is now being solved by constructing a **tidal storm dam**. Due to be completed in 1997, the dam will allow the Nieuwe Waterweg to be closed off at high tide. Rotterdam port managers hope that this will only be a rare occurrence since the port must be accessible at all times. Therefore the dykes will still be raised slightly to minimise the use of the dam.
The Nieuwe Waterweg is navigable for very large vessels and forms the backbone of the **Rotterdam ports**, stretching from the sea to the town centre 30 kilometres inland. Rotterdam is the largest seaport in the world, particularly through activities such as transshipment and storage of goods and oil refining. A current growth activity is container transport. The "Spido" boat trips which sail from Rotterdam give a good view of the port.
After the Nieuwe Waterweg was constructed the **De Beer** wildlife resort developed into a remarkable area until, in 1965, the port area and adjacent industrial estates began to be expanded with the **Maasvlakte**. This was probably the most serious attack on the ecology and environment of the dune area so far.

Hook of Holland was originally the residential area for the canal workers. The oldest, most western part of the town was demolished by the Germans during the Second World War in order to defend access to the ports of Rotterdam. Since the war, Hook of Holland has developed into a seaport and seaside resort.

Between Hook of Holland and Maassluis the route goes along the **Staalduinen** (steel dunes).

These dunes are of particular interest as they run inland directly from the coast.

The town of **Maassluis** developed around two sluices, constructed in the 14th century. Its peak of influence, in the 17th century, was based on its success as a fishing port.
Today, the most important activity is the pilotage of ships along the Nieuwe Waterweg. Nevertheless the atmosphere of this
old fishing town has been preserved, especially around the old harbour.

You cross by ferry to **Rozenburg**, which became an island due to the construction of the Nieuwe Waterweg. Later it was broken up even further when other canals and ports were dug. Apart from the residential centre the whole island has merged into the ports and industrial estates of Botlek and Europoort. Oil storage and refinery provide the overwhelming sights and smells.

The route follows the main road over three bridges: over the **Calandkanaal**, the **Hartelkanaal** and the **Brielse meer**. Standing on the first bridge, you will notice a long row of bulging concrete plates which together form a giant wind screen preventing ships from being blown out of course. In 1995 this project received the Betonprijs (Concrete Award) for

Maassluis ▶

its remarkable design.

Voorne-Putten is the most northern of the natural islands that now lie before you. The compound names of many islands reveal that they developed from the merging of more than one island.

Brielle developed from two neighbouring villages, Brielle and Maasland, on the bank of the small river Goote, which runs into the Maas. The route goes along the Voorstraat and the Nobelstraat, the site of the dyke along which the first houses were built. In the 14th century Brielle was given city status and developed into an important seaport. The star shaped wall and canal were built in the 18th century. Shortly afterwards the mouth of the Maas silted up, marking the end of an economically flourishing era. In 1951 Brielle lost its direct opening to the sea when the Maas of Brielle was dammed. However this did create the Brielse Meer which is now an important tourist area. The area surrounded by the embankment and the adjacent farmland was given protected status in 1975.

The **Voornse duinen** (dunes of Voorne) are regarded by biologists as the most beautiful dunes in the Netherlands, particularly the parts that have retained their connection to the sea. These dunes are not used for water extraction or filtration so an extremely rare and varied vegetation is able to grow. The route runs straight across the island, a patchwork of small polders, passing one of the highlights of the Voornse duinen: the **Quakjeswater,** situated north-west of the Haringvlietdam. The Quakjeswater is a dune pond at the centre of an old, natural alder wood with yellow irises, possibly a remnant of an arm of the former river Goote.

The **Haringvlietdam** is the northernmost dam of the **Delta Works**. The Delta Works project was designed to prevent the 1953 floods from recurring. When the dykes broke in 1953 large parts of

Zeeland, the islands of South Holland and Western Brabant were flooded and more than 1500 people were drowned. The Delta Works dammed up most of the tidal inlets, shortening the coastline considerably and thus reducing the danger of flooding.

On the island of **Goeree** the route follows the inner dune edge for some time. The quiet, narrow back roads are surrounded by a varied landscape of meadows, farmland, woods and remote villages. Directly west of the pier behind the first row of dunes is the **Kwade Hoek** wildlife reserve which is a primary dune valley. Unlike in many other coastal towns the coast has grown here since 1900, sometimes by up to 500 metres. On the beach, new embryo dunes were formed between which, on the mud-flats, vegetation started growing. This area is therefore also called "the green beach".

East and west of Ouddorp you pass the **Middelduinen** (Middle dunes) and the **Westduinen** (West dunes) respectively. These are old inland dunes which were not blown over by new dunes. The lime in these dunes was leached out over time. For this reason and because of intensive farming since the Middle Ages these dunes have levelled off and developed into a kind of undulating meadow.

Before being outstripped by the town of Goedereede, **Ouddorp** was the centre of the former island of Goeree. Notably the old church and its surroundings, which form the oldest part of the town, are interesting sights.

Directly west of Ouddorp are found remarkable small pieces of land surrounded by earth walls; the **Haaygemeten**. For centuries these plots were blown over and are now covered by a thick layer of sand. These earth walls ("schurvelingen") originally marked the boundaries of the plots and served at the same time as cattle fences. During the first half of the 20th century they were raised with sand dug from the plots themselves, bringing the crops closer to the ground water.

Accommodation

▬

Hotels and guest houses
16- **Brielle**, "De Zalm", Voorstraat 6, 0181-413388, ƒ80,-
17- **Ouddorp**, "Akershoek", Boompjes 1, 0187-681437, ƒ80,-
18- **Ouddorp**, "Pension de Schuur", Dorpsweg 26, 0187-681724, ƒ74,-

Nivon house
4- **Vlaardingen**, "De Hoogkamer", Van Baerlestraat 252, 010-4346811, inf: 010-4353205

Campsites
19- **Vlaardingen**, "De Hoogkamer", edge of residential area, 010-4346811 (▲)
20- **Brielle**, "De Krabbeplaat", Oude Veerdam 4, 0181-412363 (▣)
21- **Brielle**, "De Meeuw", Batterijweg 1, 0181-412777 (▣)
22- **Oostvoorne**, "Kruininger Gors", Gorsplein 2, 0181-482711 (▣)
23- **Rockanje**, "Het Waterbos", Duinrand 11, 0181-401900 (▣)
24- **Hellevoetsluis**, "De Quack", Duinweg 14, 0181-312646 (▣)
25- **Hellevoetsluis**, "'t Weergors", Zuiddijk 2, 0181-312430 (▣)
26- **Ouddorp**, "De Klepperstee", Vrijheidsweg 1, 0187-681511 (▣)

Tourist attractions

▬

Hook of Holland
Kustverlichtingsmuseum (lighting museum, in lighthouse), Willem van Houtenstraat 102
Nederlands Kustverdedigingsmuseum (sea defense), Stationsweg 82, 0174-382898/383128

Maassluis
Gemeentemuseum (municipal museum), Zuiddijk 16, 010-5913813
Nationaal Scheepvaartmuseum (shipping), Hoogstraat 1, 010-4709564

Goedereede
Torenmuseum (history of agriculture and fisheries), Domtoren, 0187-682796

Ouddorp
Raad- en polderhuis (traditional room, clog factory, archeology), Raadhuisstraat 4, 0187-681303
Bezoekerscentrum Grevelingen (visitor centre), De Punt 4, 0187-682346

Tourist Information (VVV)

▬

Hook of Holland, Hoekse Brink 23, 0174-382446
Brielle, Nobelstraat 8, 0181-413333
Ouddorp, Bosweg 2, 0187-681789

The **Brouwersdam** not only connects South Holland with Zeeland but also closes off the former **De Grevelingen** lake. This area is important both from a scenic and from a recreational point of view. The recreational facilities - mainly watersport - are concentrated on the eastern and western ends of the lake, near the dams. Windsurfing is mainly practised from the Brouwersdam and from the Veersegatdam. This is where the wind is strongest, which is much appreciated by the more advanced windsurfers and sailors. In the Grevelingen lie a few shallows which over time have run dry, allowing nature to take its course. Some places are left untouched so that the area can grow wild and eventually woods will develop. On others, cattle, horses and sheep are kept to prevent the area from growing wild.

On the northern point of the Brouwersdam we find **De Punt van Goeree**, a natural park and recreational resort. Part of De Punt van Goeree consists of dunes which have lost contact with the sea since the dam was built. Behind this is an area which has run dry and has partly been forested. The **Visitor centre** has exhibits about the past and present of De Grevelingen as well as the **Trammuseum** which moved from Hellevoetsluis to

De Punt in 1988. This is the starting point of a five kilometre long steam tramline along the Brouwersdam to the **Kabbelaarsbank**. The Kabbelaarsbank used to be a shallow in the mouth of the Grevelingen. At the end of the 1980s, **Port Zélande**, a holiday village with marinas and windsurfing facilities, was developed on the Kabbelaarsbank.

We now enter the province where the traditional Dutch battle against the sea is most obvious: **Zeeland**. This province was hard hit by the floods of 1953 and the Delta Works which were built in response to the disaster have changed the area significantly. But the battles waged against the sea in previous centuries have also left their traces.

Originally, the town of **Ellemeet** was situated two kilometres south east of its current position, at the junction between the Schelpweg and the Hogeweg, along which the route runs. The only thing left of this former town is the cemetery. After the Reformation Ellemeet was moved to a higher area, because the area on which it was built had become too swampy. Most interesting is the old **village forge** with a "travalje" outside the door. Horses were placed in a travalje while they were shod.

▼ Grevelingen dyke near Scharendijke

Serooskerke is one of the most characteristic "ring villages" in Zeeland. The Gothic church with its leaning tower, at the centre of the churchyard, is surrounded by a ring of streets.

Just south of Serooskerke we reach **Schelphoek**. This area was lost to the sea after the 1953 floods. The route follows the former dyke, one kilometre to the south, which has an opening of no less than 500 metres. Since the floods, this has become a valuable wildlife area. Along the bank of the Eastern Scheldt between Serooskerke and Westenschouwen you pass several **Inlagen**, small strips of land between the seadyke and another further inland which serves as a reserve dyke. Along the coast runs a deep inlet with a strong undercutting current. This inlet has already caused many dykes to succumb and many former "inlagen" to be lost to the sea. The inner dykes were built with earth from the "inlagen". They are therefore relatively low and swampy and attract many birds. Along the Koudekerkse inlaag is the **Plompetoren**, the former church tower of the village of Koudekerke which was lost to the water.

Between Schouwen-Duiveland and Noord-Beveland is the **Stormvloedkering** (storm tide dam), the most prestigous project carried out under the Delta Works programme. The dam was completed in 1986 and has been open to traffic since 1987. In order to preserve the unique natural environment in the Eastern Scheldt (mud-flats, underwater life) which requires tidal movement, this dam was built so as to allow sea water to run through, at an additional cost of six million guilders (appr. £2.4 m). The dam now has three openings which, in an emergency, can be closed with enormous sluices. This dam is a true technological masterpiece, requiring many technological innovations which may never actually be used again.
On the former working island of **Neeltje Jans** there is a permanent exhibition about the Delta Works. There are also trips that take you within the storm tide dam itself.

Between Noord-Beveland and Walcheren the route goes along the **Veersegatdam**, the first dam built under the Delta Works programme and completed in 1961. Behind the dam the **Veerse Meer** (Lake Veere) was created. Long stretches of shore were developed for recreational use, particularly watersports. From the dam you have a good view of the lake and the towers of the former fortified town of **Veere** which fortunately has been able to keep its historical charm.

On Walcheren we still find a number of **Vliedbergen**, some of which you pass near Gapinge. Just south of the church is a vliedberg which has partly been excavated and another, purer example lies just north east of the village. Chapter three describes the vliedbergen in more detail. 600 metres north of the latter vliedberg is the moat of the former Gapinge castle. The village of Gapinge still has a mediaeval church in perfect condition. It is claimed that this is the most beautiful church in Walcheren.

Between Gapinge and Middelburg the route passes the cemetery of the former village of **Schellach**, of which nothing remains but a slight raising of the fields.

Accommodation

NJHC hostel
7- **Oostkapelle**, "Kasteel Westhove", Duinvlietweg 8, 0118-581254

Campings
27- **Renesse**, "De Wijde Blick", Hoogezoom 112, 0111-461444 ()
28- **Renesse**, "Prinsenhoeve", Hoogenboomlaan 19, 0111-461685 ()
29- **Burgh-Haamstede**, "Ginsterveld", J.J. Boeijesweg 45, 0111-651590 ()
30- **Oostkapelle**, "Ons Buiten", Aagtekerkseweg 2a, 0118-581813 ()
31- **Veere**, Het Veerse Gat", Landschuurweg 5, 0118-501432 ()

Tourist Attractions

Ouddorp
RTM Grevelingen (tram museum, transport in early 20th century), De Punt West, 0187-683052
Grevelingen Visitor Centre De Punt 4, 0187-682346

Scharendijke
Round trips on Grevelingen, inf: 0111-414631

Neeltje Jans
Delta-Expo (Delta Works, 2000 years water engineering), Oosterscheldedam, 0111-652702
Fishing in the North Sea inf: 0111-481505/652046

Oostkapelle
Zeeland biological museum Duinvlietweg 6, 0118-582620
Fossil museum (images of prehistoric animals), Molenweg 36, 0118-582295

Veere
De Schotse huizen (the Scottish houses, merchant houses with costumes and folklore), Kaai 25-27, 0118-50744
De Vierschaar (objects of justice), Markt 5, 0118-501951
Round trips on Lake Veere
Toren O.L.- Vrouwekerk (church tower), Oudestraat

Tourist Information (VVV)

Renesse, De Zoom 17, 0111-462120
Vrouwenpolder, Dorpsdijk 19, 0118-591577
Oostkapelle, Duinweg 2a, 0118-592910
Veere, Oudestraat 28, 0118-501365

The town of **Middelburg** was built in the ninth century around a castle which itself was built as a defence against the Vikings. Where the castle once stood is now an abbey complex featuring the 85 metre high tower called Lange Jan. The clergy disappeared from the abbey in 1575 when William of Orange occupied Middleburg. Now it is the home of the municipal council.

From the 15th century Middelburg grew strongly. The Zwin silted up and the Western Scheldt became the most important route to Antwerp. By the end of the 16th and early 17th century Middelburg was the second most important town in the northern Netherlands after Amsterdam. Trade to the Dutch East and West Indies contributed heavily to this prosperity.

When in 1940 the Netherlands surrendered to Germany, Zeeland refused, as reinforcements were still feasible from France. On May 12th, therefore, the Luftwaffe bombed the town heavily, causing a fire which destroyed most of the town centre. On May 18th, Zeeland felt compelled to surrender. After the war Middelburg was reconstructed in much the same form as before. The "Delft" architectural style was used, based on old architecture.

Despite the damage, Middelburg is still the third richest town in the Netherlands in terms of heritage, after Amsterdam and Maastricht. Many monuments have been restored over the past few decades. North of the town centre you pass **Het Molenwater** park (the water of the mill) with the **Miniatuur Walcheren**, an exhibition of scale models of many buildings typical of Walcheren.

Het Molenwater was originally a holding basin which filled up at high tide. At low tide a tidal water mill was powered by the withdrawing water.

The beautiful **Damplein** is also on the route. This square was built after a block of monumental buildings was demolished to create more car parking spaces (!). The square features a reconstruction of the Korenbeurs (corn market) of 1767, a roof built on pillars. It now covers a stage where since 1975 a number of artists have laid stones in the pavement.

The route goes near the **Markt** (market) with its impressive town hall. The square was destroyed during the bomb attack of 1949 and during the reconstruction it was altered significantly. Only the

town hall was reconstructed in its original style. Every Thursday there is a market on the square. It is also the heart of the entertainment centre.

On the Houtkaai/Stationsstraat crossroads you pass the western starting point of the **LF13, the Scheldt-Rhein Route**, which runs from here to Venlo and to Duisburg in Germany. A route guide is obtainable from the Stichting Landelijk Fietsplatform.

Between Middelburg and Vlissingen you follow the Kanaal door Walcheren (Walcheren canal) which was constructed in 1873, at the same time as the railway opposite, to connect Middleburg with Vlissingen. Half way is the town of **Souburg** which

has now merged with Vlissingen. Souburg, like Middelburg, was built around a castle. The round grounds of the castle are easily recognisable behind the shopping centre.

▲ **Lange Jan, Middelburg**

The two most important economic sectors for Vlissingen are industry and tourism, both of them are linked to the town's coastal location. Within the industrial sector, shipbuilding and the nuclear plant near Borssele are both highly dependent on the water.

The centre of Vlissingen, right on the seafront, is full of life with plenty of entertainment and many monuments. Recently the boulevard was thoroughly refurbished which gave tourism a new boost. At the end of the boulevard is a wind harp made of bamboo pipes, like the one in Petten.

The **Western Scheldt** is the only channel into Zeeland not closed by a dam, because it is an important shipping route to Antwerp. You therefore cross by **ferry** to the fishing port of Breskens in Flemish Zeeland.

Flemish Zeeland has its own, already slightly Belgian, character. No doubt this is because the area is shut off from the rest of the Netherlands by the sea whereas there are no barriers between Flemish Zeeland and Belgium. As a result, many people who live here have more contact with Belgium than with the rest of the Netherlands.

The first part of the route through Flemish Zeeland goes along the coast. This coast has very few dunes which are very narrow and often have a dyke behind them.

Along the coast, there are several small seaside resorts serving larger towns more inland. **Cadzand-Bad** is the largest, oldest and best known coastal town in this area. The beach between Cadzand and the Zwin is known for the prehistoric fossils such as shark's teeth which sometimes wash ashore.

The coast of Flemish Zeeland has two important wildlife areas. Both are mud-flats behind a narrow strip of dunes with an opening which, at high tide, lets the sea water through. The most eastern of the two, the **Verdronken Zwarte Polder** (drowned black polder), was created after a breach in the dyke. The dune strip was deposited in the lee of the broken dyke. More to the west is the mainly Belgian **Zwin**, the mouth of the tidal creek which once was an important shipping route to Bruges but has now silted up.

Near the Verdronken Zwarte Polder the route leaves the coast and runs inland to **Cadzand**, the centre of the former island with the same name. During the Eighty Years' War this was one among

few towns in West Flemish Zeeland which were not flooded. It has therefore kept its original form, a church in a ring.

Near Terhofstede the route crosses a road which reaches the village of **Retranchement** a kilometre further north. This village is well worth a visit. During the Eighty Years' war the building of a garrison town was started but building stopped when a truce was concluded for 12 years (1609-1621). When the truce ended the front had moved so far that there was no longer a need to complete it. It therefore developed into a normal village. The fortifications are magnificent, and beautifully adorned with luxuriant vegetation.

Terhofstede is an old farming settlement at the edge of the former island of Cadzand.

North of Sluis the route crosses over a cove which was created by the sea when the land was deliberately flooded during the Eighty Years' War. Further south, to the southeast of the route, are the foundations of the **Kasteel van Sluis** (Sluis castle) which was built at the end of the 14th century to keep an eye on ships on their way to Bruges. It was demolished by the French in 1794.

The town of Sluis developed as a seaport at the time of Bruges' predominance. After the Zwin silted up it lost its importance as a seaport. In 1944 the town was destroyed during heavy fighting between German and Allied troops. The **Stadhuis** (Town Hall) is the only building that was restored in its former state. The Flemish belfort with its four towers, a symbol of the autonomy of a city, is the most characteristic part of this building and gives Sluis a traditional charm. The **Vestingwerken** (fortifications) with their austere design, last improved in 1702, are another remarkable element. Today, Sluis is a popular day trip destination with Flemish people from Belgium. The sex shops were once a major attraction, although this sector of the local economy has been more constrained of late.

Accommodation

Hotels and guest houses

19- **Vlissingen**, "Ineke", Paul Krugerstraat 140, 0118-412410, ƒ 80,-
20- **Vlissingen**, "Wolff", Aagje Dekenstraat 95-97, 0118-414797, ƒ 80,-
21- **Vlissingen**, "Royal", Badhuisstraat 3, 0118-412201, ƒ 90,-
22- **Breskens**, "Het Wapen van Breskens", Grote Kade 33, 0117-381401, ƒ 135,-
23- **Breskens**, "Scaldis", Langeweg 3, 0117-382420, ƒ 140,-
24- **Sluis**, "Le Provincal", Sint Jansstraat 10, 0117-462187, ƒ 75,-
25- **Sluis**, "Sanders de Paauw", Kade 42, 0117-461224, ƒ 80,-

Campsites

32- **Breskens**, "Napoleonhoeve", 't Zandertje 30, 0117-381428 ( )
33- **Groede**, "De Blikken", Barendijk 3, 0117-371365 ( )
34- **Nieuwvliet**, "Zonneweelde", Baantspoldersedijk 1, 0117-371910 ( )
35- **Retranchement**, "De Wildhof", Kanaalweg 4/5, 0117-391406 ( )
36- **Sluis**, "De Meidoorn", Hoogstraat 68, 0117-461662 ( )

Tourist Attractions

Middelburg
Miniatuur Walcheren
Koepoortlaan 1, 0118-612525
Zeeuws Museum (art, archeology, tapestery), Abdij 3, 0118-626655
Ramschip Schorpioen (oldest naval ship in the Netherlands), Loskade, 0118-639649/413297
Historama(audio-visual history presentation), Abdij 9, 0118-616448

Vlissingen
Reptielenzoo "Iguana"
Bellamypark 35, 0118-417219
Stedelijk Museum (town history), Bellamypark 19, 0118-412498

St. Jacobstoren (55 metre tower), Oude Markt
Round trips on the Western Scheldt
Maritiem attractiecentrum Het Arsenaal (naval, submarine and shipwreck simulator), Arsenaalplein 1, 0118-415400
Laser-action (high-tech laser game), Voltaweg 7, 0118-464300

Breskens
Visserijmuseum (fisheries museum), Kaai 1, 0117-383656
Round trips on the Western Scheldt

Sluis
Stadhuis/belfore (35 metre tower, art and archeology), Grote Markt 1, 0117-475500

Tourist Information (VVV)

Middelburg, Markt 65, 0118-616851
Vlissingen, Nieuwendijk 15, 0118-412345
Breskens, Boulevard 14, 0117-381888
Cadzand-Bad, Boulevard de Wielingen 44d, 0117-391298
Sluis, St. Annastraat 15, 0117-461700

▲ Ferry on the Western Scheldt   53

Sluis - Oudenburg

The first part of this stage mainly runs on the tow-path along the **Kanaal Brugge-Sluis**, also called the **Damse Vaart** or **Napoleonkanaal**. Napoleon ordered the canal dug when Antwerp was blockaded during the war with England, which created the need for a waterway between Dunkerque and Antwerp. Canals already existed between Dunkerque and Bruges but a connection between Bruges and the Scheldt was still needed. As the Zwin formerly assured this connection it was decided to use its bed, which had silted up, as the course for the new canal. It was planned to construct the canal as far as Breskens but this goal was never achieved. When Belgium separated from the Netherlands in 1830 the project was stopped. It had at this point progressed as far as Sluis.
The canal, bordered with poplars, runs through an open landscape. The small towns and villages in this area date from the era when the Zwin was still an important waterway. After it silted up at the end of the Middle Ages the towns and villages lost their power and collapsed.
Today, those which still exist are no more than modest but very charming polder villages.

One kilometre west of the Dutch-Belgian border in the direction of Hoeke, the route passes a number of concrete constructions, the remains of bunkers and fortifications from the First World War. On these grounds the **Fort Sint Donaas** once stood. After Sluis was conquered by the Dutch in 1604 this fort was built by Spain to obstruct the trade route between Sluis and Bruges, as at this point the freight from sea-going ships had to be transferred to ships from Bruges.
After Belgian independence the fort lost its importance and was demolished. Around the former fort are several ponds which were created by the extraction of clay for the production of bricks.

The first village you come to in Belgium is **Hoeke**. Its 13th century **church** of St. Jacob de Meerdere recalls the days of former glory.

Oostkerke also has a 13th century church, the **Sint-Kwintenskerk** with its typical angular tower. Just outside the village you can still see the contours of a mediaeval **castle.**

The village of **Monnikerede**, which used to be situated between Hoeke and Oostkerke in the 19th century, was destroyed and the land dug up when the canal was constructed.

Parallel to the Damse Vaart between Hoeke and Oostkerke runs the **Krinkeldijk**. The route leaves the canal bank to follow this dyke for a short while. The dyke was constructed in the 11th century along the former tidal cove of the Zwin and served as a sea defence.

Half way between Sluis and Bruges the course of the Damse Vaart is interrupted by two canals parallel to each other divided by a small strip of land. The most eastern of the two, he **Leopoldkanaal** drains off clean water from the polders, the other, the **Schipdonkkanaal** drains off the polluted water from the Leie. Therefore, they are also called the Blinker (shiner) and the Stinker (which needs no translation).

Having rejoined the tow-path along the channel the route passes the small town of **Damme**. This town is situated south of the Damse Vaart, but as the canal was dug straight through the star-shaped fort its remnants lie on both sides of the channel. Damme has never lost its old charm, from the days when it was a commercial town. Now it is a flourishing tourist town. There is a statue of **Tijl Uilenspiegel**, the fictional character who challenged the Spaniards during the Eighty Years'

▲ **Damme**
photo: WVT

War; in the story, Damme was his place of birth. The moats of the fortress have silted up and are now covered with vegetation. Part of the old walls of the former fortress are now a nature reserve.
Outside this picturesque village the route passes the **Sint Kristoffelhoeve** (St Christopher's farm) and the **Scellemolen** (Mill of Scelle).

Just before reaching Bruges there is a small wood with the ruin of the old **fort van Beieren**, built in 1701 during the War of the Spanish Succession. Aerial photos still clearly show the star-shaped pattern of the fort. The ruin now has the status of a national monument.

Through the Dampoort you reach the outskirts of the historic town of **Bruges**. In the ninth century a fortified castle was built on the place which is now called Burg. The town used to have a direct connection to the sea via the Zwin as far as Damme, and from there by the river Rije, and could thus develop into an important seaport. In the 13th century Bruges was one of the most important European craft and trade centres. In the 15th century the town went into decline when the Zwin silted up and Antwerp took over its position. In the 17th century Bruges won back some of its importance by developing new crafts such as the lace industry and because many administrative functions were established here. With its many canals, its cobbled roads and its historic buildings, Bruges is an extremely beautiful Flemish town full of character.

From Bruges, the route runs west along the **Ghent-Bruges-Ostend canal**. This canal was also constructed after a natural sea-inlet was blockaded for military reasons, when the northern Netherlands had freed themselves from Spanish control and blockaded the Zwin/Scheldt estuary. The canal was to give Bruges, Ghent and other towns a new connection to the sea and largely followed the course of the river Ieperlee which ran between Ieper and Bruges. The Ieperlee was made navigable by deepening, broadening and straightening it. Other parts were newly dug.

The area immediately west of Bruges and south of the canal is a higher area, grown with woods. During the predominance of Bruges many castles and country estates were built here. Parts of these country estates and adjacent gardens still exist in the outskirts and suburbs of Bruges.
From the route we can see the **Waggelwater** with

the castle of **Norenburg**, situated on the edge of Bruges. The Waggelwater was created in the first half of the 20th century when sand was extracted for the building of the dyke on which the Bruges-Blankeberge railway was constructed. The surroundings of the pond were afforested and are now popular for walking.

Further westward the channel runs through a low and swampy area which used to be a peat bog. When the peat was dug, the area was surrounded by dykes and the land impoldered. Being swampy, this area has a varied, lush vegetation and is very popular with birds. First, you pass the **Meetkerkse Moere** on the other side of the channel. Its wettest part used to be colonised by ducks, but is now a nature reserve hosting a heronry.

Between Stalhillebrug and Ostend the land is slightly higher. There is a remarkable variation of farmland between the higher areas near the coast and the meadows behind on the wet **Poelgronden**. Levelling of the landscape makes these combinations of habitats increasingly rare. This landscape developed through the "reversal of the contours" which took place after the sea had withdrawn. This process is described in chapter four.

Near Plassendalebrug, several kilometres before reaching Ostend, the route turns through 90 degrees near the sluices and leads along the **Kanaal Plassendale-Nieuwpoort**. In 1638 it was decided to dig the canal when the old connection between Plassendale and Ostend could no longer be used because of tidal movements. It was therefore decided also to build the rest of the connection, between Bruges and Dunkerque, inland. The canal was completed in 1661. Initially it was well used, but its depth became less and less adequate. Today, the channel is very popular with anglers.

Accommodation

Hotels and guest houses

26- **Hoeke**, "Welkom", Damse Vaart Noord 34, 050-602492

27- **Damme**, "De Gulden Kogge", Damse Vaart Zuid 12, 050-35421

28- **Brugge**, "De Krakele", St. Pieterskaai 63, 050-315643

29- **Brugge**, "Van Eijck", Korte Zilverstraat 7, 050-335276

30- **Brugge**, "Central", Markt 30, 050-331805

31- **Brugge**, "'t Speelmanshuys", 't Zand 3, 050-339552

32- **Jabbeke**, "Concordia", Permekelaan 3, 050-812226

Holiday farms

Damme, "De Stamper", Zuiddijk 12, 050-500197

Stahille, "Hove ter Hille", Nachtegaalstraat 46, 050-811197

Youth hostel

8- **Brugge**, "Bauhaus Int. Youth Hotel", Langestraat 135, 050-341093

9- **Brugge**, "Snuffel Sleep Inn", Ezelstraat 49, 050-333133

10- **Brugge**, "Europa Jeugdherberg", Baron Ruzettelaan 143, 050-352679

Campsites

37- **Hoeke**, "Hoeke", Damse Vaart Oost 10, 050-500496

38- **Sint-Michiels (Brugges)**, "Sint-Michiel", Tillegemstraat 55, 050-380819

39- **Sint-Kruis (Brugges-West)**, "Memling", Veltemweg 109, 050-355845 ( )

40- **Jabbeke**, "Klein Strand", Varsenareweg 29, 050-811440

Tourist Attractions

Damme

Stadhuis (historic town hall), Marktplein, 050-361496

Museum St. Janshospitaal (religious objects, furniture), Kerkstraat 33, 050-354621

Scellemolen
Damse Vaart-West

Also:
Huize St Jan, Tijl Uilenspiegl monument, St Kristoffelhoeve

Brugges

H. Bloedbasiliek (basilica), Burg, 050-316529

Groeninge museum (schilderkunst)
Dijver 12, 050-339911

Gruuthusemuseum (tapestry, sculpture, etc.), Dijver 17, 050-339911

O.L.- Vrouwekerk (Michelangelo Virgin), Mariastraat

Also:
Halle and Belfort, historic town hall, museum Brugse Vrije, Minnewater, Brangwijnmuseum, St. Jan-hospitaal, Memlingmuseum, St.Salvator church

Tourist Information

Damme, Stadhuis (town hall), Markt, 050-353319

Brugges, Burg 11, 050-448686

Jabbeke, Dorpsstraat 3, 050-812181

▲ **Damse Vaart**
photo: WVT

Oudenburg - Diksmuide

The northernmost town on the Plassendale-Nieuwpoort canal is **Oudenburg**. A number of roman sites have been excavated in Oudenburg among which are the foundations of a "castellum".
From the 12th until the 14th century Oudenburg was in its heyday, as a centre of the textile industry. In the 15th century Bruges began to dominate this sector and Oudenburg went into decline.

After the "Nieuwebrug" bridge near the village of **de Verloren Kost** the route temporarily leaves the canal and crosses the disused Ostend-Torhout railway, now a cycle and foot path. Following this path towards Ostend the route goes through an area characterised by creeks, formed at the end of the 16th century during the siege of Ostend. Dunes were dug up for strategic reasons which allowed the sea to penetrate inland, giving the area its typical form. Since then, it has developed naturally and is now a protected landscape. After this pleasant little detour you will rejoin the route just past the **Snaaskerke** brickyard.

Four kilometres further on we reach **Leffinge**. The 55 metre neo-gothic church tower rises above the town and can be seen well before we reach it. In the vicinity of the town many roman relics and traces of old fortifications have been found. The main attraction however is the **Fleriskothoeve**, an ancient farm formerly belonging to the order of the Knights Templars. Its typical Frisian barn is a very characteristic feature. This and several other farms, some of them fortified, give Leffinge its typical rural charm.

The route crosses the Torhoutse Steenweg and rejoins the canal near the Kalsijdebrug. Past Leffingebrug it passes a marsh, once a very important habitat for amphibians, called the **Puydebroeken**. The area used to flood in the winter creating a favourable environment for frogs. Drainage of the ground has damaged this habitat, although a remarkable flora and fauna have remained.

Five kilometres west of Leffinge, past Slijpebrug, the route leaves the canal again and heads towards the coast. If you want to visit the

seaside, you should detour to **Westende** as the route is only two kilometres from the beach here. The town of Westende developed in the 11th century west of a wide strip of land called "Ter Streep". This piece of land used to be a mud-flat between the sea and the Testerep waterway. In 1173 the abbey of Oudenburg started building dykes and cultivating the land. Around that time many farms were built, some of which still exist such as the **Grote Bamburg** and the **Vlaming Hofstede**. Since the 19th century Westende has developed as a seaside resort. The wide beach (400 metres at low tide) is especially popular.

The route continues towards de

▲ **Abbey farm, Oudenburg**
photo: WVT

59

history of the Netherlands is the battle in Nieuwpoort in 1600, between the armies of the United Provinces commanded by prince Maurits and those of Spain commanded by Spinola.

In 1914 the plain of the Yser was flooded to cut off the German troops, completely destroying the town. After 1918 it was rebuilt in its traditional style.

At Nieuwpoort the route makes a 90 degree turn inland. It now goes along the Plassendale-Diksmuide canal and onto a cycle and foot path built on the **disused railway from Nieuwpoort to Diksmuide**. The area between the railway and the river Yser shows many traces of the "battle of the Yser". In order to cut off the German advance into France the whole area was flooded on 29 October 1914 by opening the Veurne-Ambachtsas (a sluice) at Nieupoort. After a Belgian counter offensive the Germans pulled back behind the Yser which marked the beginning of four years of heavy and bloody fighting. Many monuments, memorial stones, bunkers and war cemeteries in the polder villages along the route serve as a reminder of those dreadful times.

Two kilometres south of Nieuwpoort the route reaches **Ramskapelle**, a village which was completely destroyed during the First World War. Of the Mediaeval abbeys, which played an important part in the impoldering of the area, only the foundations remained.

The village of **Pervijze**, situated five kilometres south of Ramskapelle, was also completely destroyed during the First World War and had to be rebuilt after 1918.

After the Grote Beverdijkvaart, several kilometres before Diksmuide, the route leaves the disused railway path. It now reaches the **Dodengang**, a reconstruction of a position on the Yser war front. The Belgian and the German trenches sometimes lay only 50 metres from each other. For four years the two armies faced each other across that tiny strip of land. Commanders on both sides were content to wager large sums in blood for negligible territorial gain.

Schuddebeurze. To your left you see a **bunker complex**, remnants of the German Atlantic Wall. Via the Boterdijk we reach the small seaside town of **Lombardsijde** which used to be a flourishing seaport in the 11th century. On 23 June 1116 a flood washed away almost the entire town and a violent storm in 1134 also caused enormous damage. Subsequently most of the inhabitants moved to Santhooft, later renamed Nieuwpoort. These were not the only ordeals Lombardsijde had to face. After being severely damaged during the First World War and rebuilt afterwards, it was struck in 1965 by a great flood. Today, Lombardsijde is a quiet holiday resort and very popular with campers.

The town of **Nieuwpoort** was founded in 1163 after the area, which was inundated during the Dunkirk III transgression, was protected by dykes. On the edge of the reclaimed land, towns and ports were founded by Count Filips van den Elzas. Novus Portus (latin for new port - Nieuwpoort) was one of these towns. After it was given city rights walls and gates were built and moats were dug. The town grew rapidly with the growth of the ports. After 1270 Nieuwpoort developed into a fishing port, and entered its most flourishing period in the 15th century. Situated strategically at the mouth of the river IJzer, Nieuwpoort has had a history of sieges and battles. One of the most famous battles in the

▲ **Church in Nieuwpoort**

Accommodation

Hotels
33- **Oudenburg**, "Oude Abdijhoeve", Marktstraat 1, 059-265167
34- **Nieuwpoort**, "Duinhotel", Albert I-laan 101, 058-233154/233366
35- **Nieuwpoort**, "Sandeshoved", Zeedijk 26, 058-234153/238523
36- **Nieuwpoort**, "De l'IJzer", Sluizen 10, 058-233383
37- **Nieuwpoort**, "Pacific", Albert I-laan 97, 058-234034
38- **Nieuwpoort**, "Uilenspiegel", Albert I-laan 159, 058-237069
39- **Nieuwpoort**, "Regina", Albert I-laan 137, 058-233366

Holiday farms
Nieuwpoort, "'t Klein Noordhof", Diksmuidseweg 14, 058-234816
Leffinge, "Ten Hullenhove", Leenstraat 2, 059-701158

Youth hostel
11- **Oostduinkerke**, "De Peerdevisser", Dorpsstraat 19, 058-512649

Campsites
41- **Bredene (East-Ostend)**, "Zandpolder", Zandstraat 103, 059-320036
42- **Lombardsijde**, "Zomerzon", Elizabethlaan 1, 058-237396
43- **Lombardsijde**, "De Lombarde", Elizabethlaan 4, 058-236839
44- **Lombardsijde**, "KACB", Bassevillestraat 81, 058-237343
45- **Westende**, "Ever Green", Lombardsijdelaan 171, 058-234804
46- **Nieuwpoort**, "Nieuwpoort", Brugsesteenweg 49, 058-236037

Tourist Attractions

Oudenburg
Oude Abdijhoeve (old abbey farm, local beer), Marktstraat 1, 051-503814
Stedelijk museum (roman relics), Marktstraat 25, 059-266027

Nieuwpoort
Koning Albert I-monument
Kustweg, 058-235587
Vismijn (fish market) Kaai, 058-233364
Round trips at sea and on the river Yser
Children's farm, Elf-Juliewijk, 058-236986

Tourist Information

Oudenburg, Weststraat 24, 059-266027
Nieuwpoort, Marktplein 7, 058-235594
Veurne-Ambacht, Goudenhoofdstraat 19, 058-299479
Veurne, Grote Markt 29, 058-312154
Middelkerke, Casselaan 4, 059-300368
Westende, Jasparlaan 173, 059-302085

The town of **Diksmuide** developed in the seventh century on the former estuary of the river Yser. The town came to its height in the 12th century and was the third most important Flemish town and a centre of the textile industry. When the Yser channel silted up and the town of Nieuwpoort was founded Diksmuide slowly went into decline. The town blossomed again as a recognised centre for dairy produce to which it owes the nickname "Butter town".

Diksmuide too was destroyed during the First World War but was rebuilt in its original style after the war. The 50 metre high **IJzertoren** (IJzer or Yser tower) was built in 1928 in memory of the many Flemish soldiers who died here during the war. The tower was blown up in 1946 and replaced by a new, 83 metre high one in 1965, situated behind the remnants of the original tower. Apart from being a peace monument and a watch tower it is also a place of pilgrimage for Flemish Nationalists, to whom it recalls in particular the fate of Flemish conscripts whose deaths occurred under French speaking officers.

On this stage the route runs beside or close to the river Yser. Via the river's west bank, the IJzerdijk, it goes to **St. Jacobskapelle**, another village completely destroyed in the war. It developed around the 13th century **chapel** which like the rest of the village was rebuilt in its original style after the war. The church and its surroundings were given the status of "precious landscape" in 1974.

Further south and west the route passes through an open landscape of ditches and dispersed farms. Several kilometres after Nieuwkapelle on the south-east side of the canal the **Blankaart-spaarbekken** (reservoir) comes into view, a striking element in this landscape. The reservoir, set in a seven metre high octagonal concrete basin, is used as a drinking water facility. Together with the De Blankaart wetland reserve to the east, it attracts a wide variety of water birds, mainly in the winter when the lower areas are flooded.

▲ **Flemish stepgables**
photo: WVT

remnant of the former fortifications. There is also an old **Taxus** (yewtree) to which Julius Caesar is said once to have tied his horse. The local authorities in partnership with the local shopkeepers have tried to reinvigorate the economy of Lo by promoting it as a tourist attraction. This initiative has been a great success and in 1985 the town won back its city rights, lost during the French revolution of 1789.

The route continues along the Vaartdijk to the point where the Vaartdijk and the Lovaart flow together in **Fintele**. In Fintele a little path goes down to the bank of the Yser and leads to the **Hooipiete** (Hay bridge). This small bridge dates from 1635 and has given its name to the restaurant behind it which dates back at least to 1500. The bridge serves farmers who use it to bring hay from one side of the river to the other. Large ships can only pass by dismantling the bridge beam by beam and rebuilding it after going through.

Just before reaching the complex of bridges and sluices the route turns onto the **Lovaart** towards Veurne-Lo. The Lovaart was dug in the 12th century on the initiative of the St. Niklaas abbey in Veurne. It was designed to serve as a drainage canal when the polders were reclaimed, but later, as trade developed, was used more and more as a waterway between Veurne and the river Yser.

The route passes the **Sint-Machuitmolen** (mill), the **Hullebrug** and via the Kellenaarsbrug across the Lovaart heads towards the quiet village of **Pollinkhove**. This small village owes its name to the "Heren van Pollinc" (lords of Pollinc) who occupied the farm of that same name in the 12th century. The most interesting site is the **church** which Adriaan van Pollinck had built around 1500, and where he is buried.

From Pollinkhove the route continues at about one kilometre from the Yser. It now runs at the edge of the **plateau van Isenberge**. Until this point the meadows very much dominated the Flemish landscape. From here we see a variation of meadows and farmland. On a bright day you see the witness hills, also called the Mountains of West Flanders, across the Yser.
Having crossed the trunk road from Veurne to Ieper the route is only a few kilometres away from France. The border area is characterised by quiet and unspoilt nature ith only small villages and dispersed, picturesque old farms.

The route continues to follow the IJzerdijk. The Oude Zeedijk (old seadyke) runs to its right parallel to the road. Here the route passes the **Villa Marietta** built in 1870. During the war the so-called "mother of the front" used to live here, an 80-year old woman who visited the trenches on the back of a donkey and offered her mansion as a refuge to desperate soldiers.

500 metres further on the route passes the **Knokkebrug**, a beautiful drawbridge situated at the junction between the Yser and the Ieper-Yser canal. At this point the route also joins the signed **Vlaanderen fietsroute** (Flanders cycle route) to Maastricht.
Because of the strategic position of the Knokkebrug between Ieper and Bruges the Spaniards built a fort in 1590 on this point. Louis XIV had the fort rebuilt into a star-shaped bastion. The ground on both sides of the river Yser still shows this star-shape.

2.5 kilometres north of the route is the famous town of **Lo**, the "Pearl of the Western Region". It developed on the tip of a dune on the edge of the polders near an Augustinian abbey. In the Middle Ages the town was a cheese making centre and, like so many Flemish towns in those days, it was a centre of the textile industry.
The town of Lo has been destroyed many times. In 1382 by the people of Gent, in 1582 by the Prince of Orange and again during the First World War. Many interesting things have however been preserved: the **pastorie** (presbytery), the **duiventoren** (pigeon tower), the **St. Pieters-Hallen church** which was part of the Augustinian abbey, the **klooster van de Grauwe Zusters** (cloister of the grey sisters) with its many art collections, the old **Stadhuis** (town hall) and the 14th century **Westpoort** (west gate), a

Accommodation

Hotels and guest houses
40- **Diksmuide**, "De Polderbloem", Grote Markt 8, 051-502905
41- **Diksmuide**, "Sint Jan", Bloemmolenkaai 1, 051-500274
42- **Diksmuide**, "De Vrede", Grote Markt 35, 051-500038
43- **Kaaskerke**, "Huize De Toren", IJzerdijk 71, 051-500548
44- **Lo-Reninge**, "'t Convent", Halve Reningestraat 1, 057-400771
45- **Lo-Reninge**, "Stadhuis", Markt 1, 058-288016
46- **Lo-Reninge**, "Oude Abdij", Noordstraat 3, 058-288265
47- **Lo-Reninge**, "Het Trefcentrum", Markt 11, 058-288204

Holiday farms
Diksmuide, "Hedera", Grote Markt 27, 051-510923
Stuivekenskerke (Diksmuide), "Kasteelhoeve Viconia", Kasteelstraat 2, 051-555230
Lo-Reninge, "Briesland", Oude-Kapellesteenweg 18, 058-288109
Lo-Reninge, "Ter Cnokke", Hazewind 4, 058-288956

Youth hostels
12- **Vleteren**, "De Sceure", Veurnestraat 4, 057-400901

Campsite
47- **Sint-Jacobskapelle**, "De IJzerhoeve", Kapellestraat 4, 051-500432

Tourist Attractions

Diksmuide
Dodengang,
IJzerdijk 65, 051-503814
Stadhuis en Belfort (town hall),
Markt
IJzermonument en Vredesmuseum,
IJzerdijk 49, 051-500286
Stedelijk Museum voor Diamant en Heemkunde, (city museum), Wilgendijk 55, 051-503675

Lo-Reninge
St.-Pietersabdijkerk (abbey),
Noordtraat
Stadhuis (town hall),
Markt 1
Westpoort (Westgate)
Duiventoren (pigeon tower),
Noordstraat
Museum Old Timer,
Tempelare 12,
057-400100

Tourist Information

Diksmuide, Grote Markt 28, 051-503814
Lo-Reninge, Ooststraat 1, 058-2891661

Lo
photo: WVT ▶

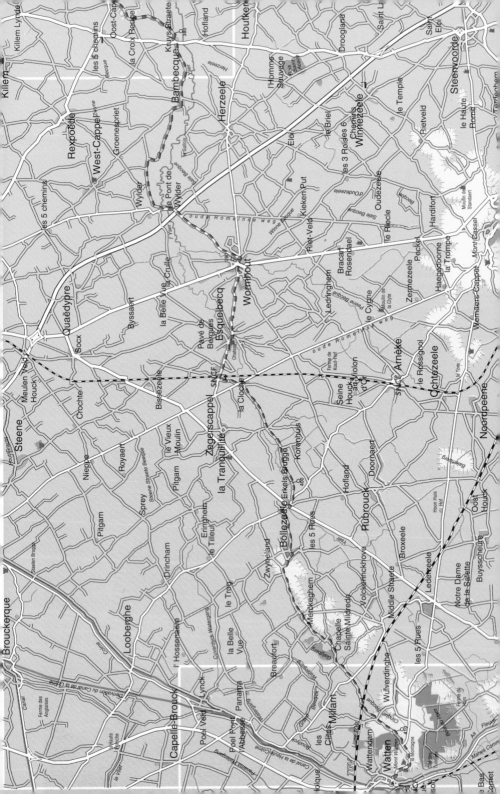

Around Oost-Cappel the North Sea Route runs for several kilometres along the Franco-Belgian border. Between 1813, when the Netherlands became an independent kingdom after the French occupation, and 1839, when Belgium separated from the Netherlands, this line used to be the border between the Netherlands and France. Several **border posts** from 1819 still stand along the route. One of those posts can be found near a tree just past the chapel on the Rue Mitoyenne/Hoge Seine junction; the route passes a second post just before the church of Oost-Cappel.

This stage of the route runs through the **Houtland**. The area, which owzes its name to the many woods which cover the area, is part of French Flanders. The Flemish influence is still present in the names of places, towns and inscriptions. Until some 350 years ago the area as far as the river Somme was part of Flanders.

Oost-Cappel is a tiny village on the border. It has a small Flemish-Gothic church, the oldest parts of which date from the 17th century.

Several kilometres south of Oost-Cappel the route reaches the valley of the river **Yser**. We have already seen this river near Nieuwpoort and Diksmuide where it is a rather wide river. Here, closer to its source, it is only a few metres wide. Along the route we find drinking wells for cattle, surrounded by trees which prevent them from drying out.

The village of **Bambeque** is situated at the point where the Yser and the Herzeelebeek flow together. The **Sint-Omaars church** dates from 1591 and has a very rich interior. We also find the remnants of the 17th century castle **kasteel Engelshof**, formerly the centre of an estate but now a farm.

In the village of **Wylder** the route crosses the **Heirweg** which, as far back as the Roman era, connected Cassel with the North Sea. The village **church** has beautifully painted woodwork. South of Wylder the route crosses the Yser, at this point nothing more than a small stream meandering through the landscape.

Crossing the **Peenebeek** the route reaches the centre of **Wormhout**, the largest village along this stage of the route. Allegedly it owes its name to the old German name of Wurm Hulta, meaning snake woods. The **Sint-Maartens church** was originally built with rubble from the abbey of Sint-Winok. The church was destroyed and rebuilt on several occasions. The present church was built in 1616 and has a baroque interior, 18th century paintings and the statue of the "weeping Madonna". It is said to have started weeping on 25 April 1406 and since then has been the object of special devotion. The **Jeanne Devos** museum is situated in the presbytery of the abbey of Vandewaele which was here from 1719 until 1761. The museum shows traditional local art and is surrounded by extensive parks.

At the centre of the square is the **Muziekkiosk** (bandstand) and just outside the village we find the **Briardmolen** from 1756, one of the oldest windmills in Flanders.

In the picturesque village of **Esquelbecq** or Ekelsbeke we cross the Yser once again. The

Esquelbecq castle ▶

central buildings are situated around the square behind the bridge: the church and the castle. The **church** is named after the evangelist Saint Folquin, who died here in 855 and was a full cousin of Charlemagne. The church, the side aisles of which are almost as tall as its nave, was built in the 16th and 17th centuries around the remnants of a 12th century Roman tower. The **castle** was rebuilt in 1606 on the same site as its predecessor and has six watchtowers and a dovecote. It is surrounded by a large "French" garden. Also, the village has several 16th, 17th and 18th century houses with typical bricklayer signs built into their facades.

The route follows the D52 for a short while, crossing the Yser once more and passing the **Bonne Aventure chapel**. From here the Chemin de la Cloche runs at a short distance from the Yser. Along the road are numerous drinking pools for cattle.

As in Wormhout, the Madonna has made an appearance in **Bollezeele**. The town has been a place of pilgrimage ever since her appearance. The object of worship is a statue of the Madonna in the church which dates from 1606. The 60 metre church tower can be seen at some distance.

Between Bollezeele and Merckegem the route goes along the **Ravensberg**, a row of hills varying in height from 50 to 60 metres. The hills are at the edge of the Flemish lowland, just a few metres above sea level. Millions of years ago the sea reached the foot of the Ravensberg. The sea here is also known as the Diestiaan Zee as it once reached Diest, situated to the west of the Ardennes in Belgium. Looking over the lowland we see Dunkerque and (to its west) Gravelines which has a nuclear power station with no less than six reactors. The many electric cables dominating the landscape carry power from the plant to the city of Lille.

East of **Merckeghem** the route passes two

pillars and a crumbled wall which were both once part of the **Cistercian convent of Ravensberg**, which was established here from 1142 to 1792.

One kilometre south west of the **water tower** a path bordered by oaks runs to the **Sint-Mildredkapel** (chapel of Saint Mildred) from 1702. The chapel lies in a little green valley on the edge of the **De Galgberg woods** where the convicted used to be hanged. The chapel is named after the English princess Mildred who travelled through France in the seventh century. At the end of her journey she waited in the nearby village of Millam - on the edge of the swampy lowland - for the sea to be calm enough to sail back to England. She waited for a whole year which she filled by taking care of children suffering from marsh fever. After her death in 725 the inhabitants of the village built the predecessor of the current chapel in memory of her good deeds. For a long time it was a place of pilgrimage for people suffering from marsh fever who prayed to the canonized princess for recovery.

At the crossroads with the road to Millam the route passes the **Matheus Caenen chapel** which, like the Saint Mildred chapel, has a Flemish inscription. Matheus Caenen had the chapel built in memory of his second wife.
Just over one kilometre westward the route crosses the **TGV line** between Lille and Calais which links to the Channel Tunnel to England. TGV means Train à Grande Vitesse or high speed train: the trains travel at approximately 300 kilometres per hour.

Approaching Watten the 71 metre high **Wattenberg** (mountain of Watten) gives a panoramic view. On one side of the road is a **mill** built of bricks and wood. The mill was in operation from 1731 to 1930, used by the occupying Germans as a watchtower and restored in 1988. On the other side of the road we see the **ruin** of an old **abbey**, which from 1072 until the French revolution of 1789 was an important religious centre for English and French Augustinian monks.

▲ **Chapel of Saint Mildred**

Accommodation

Hotels and guest houses

48- **Esquelbecq**, Deroi family, Rue de la Cloche, 28.68.93.26 (gîte)

49- **Esquelbecq**, Joos family, Route de Socx, 28.62.90.09 (gîte)

50- **Bollezeele**, Dequeker family, Rue d'Eglise 92, 28.68.93.26. (gîte)

51- **Bollezeele**, "Hostellerio St-Louis", Rue de l'Eglise, 28.68.81.83 (chambres d'hôtes)

52- **Merckeghem**, Dycke family, Route de Ronsberg 6 + 10, 28.24.29.11 (gîte)

Campsites

48- **Esquelbecq**, "Camping à la ferme Joos family", 28.62.90.09

49- **Bollezeele**, "Sain-Antoine", Chemin des cinq rues, 28.68.84.18

50- **Merckegem**, "Les cent fleurs", Rue de Cassel, 28.24.29.11

51- **Volckerinckhove**, "Du moulin", Rue Reine Becque 103, 28.68.03.23

Tourist Information

Comité département du tourisme, 20.57.00.61

Bergues, 20.68.60.44

Cassel, Grand Place, 28.40.52.55

Hondschoote, 28.68.31.55

Wormhout, 45 Grand Place, 28.62.81.23

Esquelbecq, 15 Vallée de l'Yser, 28.65.63.16

▲ **Ruin of De Ravensberg convent, Merckeghem**

The town of **Watten** developed on the junction of the Roman road between Cassel and Boulogne-sur-Mer and the river Aa; its name originated from a German word meaning "ford". Its strategic position at a valley junction has made Watten a trade centre and meeting place but at the same time a border town. From the 13th to the 18th century Watten was a regular battlefield where the Flemish counts fought the English and Spain fought the French kings. Not until 1790 did Watten become part of the French Département du Nord. From a landscape point of view Watten is on a crossroads of the Houtland, the Flemish polders and the hills of the Artois.

From the Wattenberg to the **river Aa** the route drops 70 metres in height: the course of the Aa runs only just above sea level. A recreational centre near Ruminghem, a village just north of the route, is the starting point for round trips on the river Aa and other waterways in the area.
South east of Watten the **Audomarois marsh** borders the Aa on both sides. The marsh is one of the rare wetland areas in the otherwise hilly parts of France that the route passes through. It has an area of 3500 ha.
Many waterways cut through the marsh and many small lakes were formed by peat extraction activities. Many bird species are at home here among which are harriers, cormorants, ducks and several kinds of songbirds. The meadows have a varied flower cover and the ditches are full of frogs. The route cuts straight across the area, but it may be interesting to leave the route and follow the towpath south towards **Clermarais** near St. Omer, right at the heart of the marsh.

West of the tunnel under the D600 the route goes along the foot of a long chain of hills with extensive wood cover including the **Eperlecques woods**. It also passes the entrance of the **Blockhaus**, a huge bunker (10,000 m^2, 33 metres in height) which was built by the Germans in 1942/43. It was built as a launch site for V2 missiles, but due to an attack by Allied forces which caused considerable damage the plans had to be changed. The bunker was then used as a V2 assembly site as well as for the production of liquid oxygen. The entrance is easily recognisable by the armaments:

anti-aircraft guns, a bomb, a V2 missile and scrap from shot-down aircraft.

In the small settlement of **Le Mont** the route turns onto the Route d'Audruicq which leads to a height of 80 metres in the middle of the **Eperlecques woods**. Coming out of the woods towards the north you have a tremendous view of the lowland coastal strip. Further, you can still see the nuclear plant of Gravelines and, westward, Calais.

From here the route turns onto the Rue de la Panne. East of this road is a **water tower** which in fact is not a tower: constructed on high ground, it was not necessary to build a tall building to get mains pressure. Not far from here is the **Notre Dame** farm, formerly part of an abbey and carrying a large statue of the Virgin Mary on one of its facades. In the courtyard it has a pigeon tower.

East of Nordausques the route passes a **cross with three lime trees** on a junction. It used to be a French custom to mark certain points in this way. The village of **Nordausques** has a beautiful **little church**, dedicated to Saint Martin. The church has a tower with an octagonal spire. It was renovated in the 19th century but still has many original elements

City gate, Tournehem-sur-la-Hem ▶

from the 16th and 17th centuries.

The name of the village of **Tournehem-sur-la-Hem** is explained by its position on a bend (=tour) of the small river Hem. At the beginning of the second millennium a walled **castle** was built which was later surrounded with moats. The castle has been owned by many historic figures: in 1352 it was occupied by Philips the Bold, in 1377 by the English and later by Philips the Good who, in 1479 gave it to his son Antoine le Grand Bâtard (the Great Bastard - really!). His motto "Nul ne s'y frotte" (nobody minds) is marked on a two-piece stone which was found in 1820 near the ruin of the castle. The stone now serves as a doorstep in the mill on the castle grounds. Today only the gate of the castle remains, covered with plants, which serves as an entrance to the village.

The last lord of the castle built part of the **church of Saint Médard** which dominates the town. The church has parts from the 12th, 15th and 18th centuries and has a flamboyant interior with furniture and pieces of art from former abbeys in the surrounding area. A unique feature is the 18th century organ.

Last, the **town hall** from 1764 is very much worth a visit.

South west of Tournehem lies the 1200 ha (3,000 acre) **woods** with the same name, to which entry is free. Composed mainly of beech and hornbeam the woods boast a low cover of bluebells, anemone and primrose among others.

The route goes over the bridge across the Hem. Between Tournehem and Licques it parallels the river on one side and a chain of hills on the other. On top of the hills, at a height of 121 metres, is the ruin of the **Sint Louis chapel**. This chapel can be reached by taking the road up the hill at the crossroads near Guémy, turning left after just over one kilometre. From the chapel the view extends to the other side of the English Channel. The chapel itself is visible from the sea from Cap Blanc Nez (west of Calais) to Dunkerque in the east. This is why the chapel - which was originally dedicated to the Virgin Mary - used to be a place of pilgrimage for sailors. It was destroyed in 1595 during the war against Spain. The statue from the chapel as well as some valuable objects from Tournehem castle were brought to Ardres, since when Ardres is the sailors' place of pilgrimage.

In **Guémy** the beautiful **country church** is worth seeing.

The village of **Clerque** has an interesting **church** with a 12th century Roman tower, a 15th century Gothic choir and numerous statues. The white sandstone tower carries the year 1663 when it was thoroughly renovated.

At the eastern side of the village along the river Hem lie the basins of a **trout farm**. On the other side of the village is the **statue of Le Semeur** (the sower) in honour of the harvest.

The last settlement along this stage of the route is **Cahen**, where it crosses a tributary of the Hem; near the bridge is a **water mill**.

▲ **Le Semeur, Clerque**

Accommodation

Hotels and guest houses
53- **Watten**, "Poinsard family", Rue Paul Mortier, 28.68.03.05 (gîte)
54- **Eperlecques**, "Pauwels family", Château de Ganspette, 21.93.43.93
55- **Muncq Nieurlet**, "Breton family", Rue du Bourg, 21.82.79.63 (chambres d'hôtes)
56- **Recques-sur-Hem**, "Château de Cocove", Avenue de Cocove, 21.82.68.29 (chambres d'hôtes)
57- **Zouafques**, 21.83.96.77 or 21.35.61.61 (chambres d'hôtes)
58- **Audrehem**, "Lamarliere family", 693 Rue du Parc, 21.35.06.30 (chambres d'hôtes)

Campsites
52- **Watten**, "Le val joly", Rue de l'Aa, 21.88.23.26
53- **Nordausques**, "Le Relaxe", Route de Gravelines 2, 21.35.63.77

Tourist Attractions

Eperlecques
Blockhaus d'Eperlecques
(WW2 information in gigantic bunker), Eperlecques, 21.88.44.22

Tourist Information

Watten, Rue de Dunkerque, 21.88.26.04 (town hall)
Eperlecques, 4 rue de la Mairie, 21.95.66.25
Saint-Omer, Boulevard p. Guillain, 21.98.08.51/21.98.70.00

▲ **Near Guemy**

For centuries the history of **Licques** has been inextricably bound with the presence of the **abbey** which was established here from 1132 until 1771. With the coming of the French revolution the position of the abbey became increasingly difficult. It was no longer allowed to maintain the buildings or carry out work for the poor. Eventually, on 20 August 1771, against the will of the surrounding municipalities, the district and the department, the Assemblée Nationale decided to close the monastery. The inventory was sold off and the monks moved elsewhere. Subsequently, the buildings were neglected which caused the tower to collapse in 1804. It was then decided also to take down the choir and the transept. Today, only the nave from 1747 remains, which is now the **Notre-Dame church**. Nevertheless, it is still a colossal building which dominates the surroundings, accentuated by the fact that it is situated on the highest point of the village. Only two buildings of the abbey complex have been preserved, which now house the school, the town hall, a farm and the presbytery.

Licques has also been renowned for centuries as a centre of **turkey breeding**. Each year, the weekend before Christmas, Licques celebrates the renown of its turkeys and the success of its breeders with a festival and a turkey banquet: a good time to visit if you like turkey.

Furthermore there are a number of beautiful facades and old mansions to be seen in and around the village.

The route continues through the valley between the hills of the Artois and passes the **small church of Sanghen** which stands practically alone in the open field. Its tower dates from the 15th century, much like the bell which is one of the oldest in the area.

Just west of Sanghen the route crosses a small stream. The neighbouring meadows, notably in spring, are covered in flowers such as king-cups (marsh-marigold) and cuckooflower (ragged robin).

The Route d'Eclémy goes via the settlement of **Le Paradis**, indeed the scenery is heavenly, to **Alembon**. The choir of the village **church** dates from the 15th century. Its best known feature

however is the **Ventu**, a 180 metre hill north of the village with a network of footpaths which offer fantastic views.

From here to Boulogne-sur-Mer the route goes through the National Park of **Le Boulonnais**. Typical of this landscape are the hedges which separate the agricultural plots, as well as the vegetation which is fed by the calcareous soil.

South east of Alembon the route crosses a wood, the **Bois de Haut**, which in spring has a beautiful undergrowth of bluebells. South of this wood the route literally reaches its high point: right next to it is **Mont Dauphin**, at 201 metres the second highest point of the Département du Pas de Calais.

At the bottom of the hill the route runs straight through the gates of **Colembert castle**, built in 1777 and designed by the architect Giraux-Sannier. This architect designed many houses in the Boulonnais, among them the Imperial palace. Colembert castle, also called the "little Versailles of the Pas de Calais", has as many chimneys as there are months in a year, as many rooms as there are weeks in a year and as many windows as there are days. It is now occupied by a baron and unfortunately the grounds are not open to public.

In **Le Wast** the route passes the information office of the **Boulonnais National Park** in a

▲ Gate to Colembert castle   75

valley and in between the river and the road is the fortified **Luquet farm**, where in 1597 Michel Patras de Campaigno, nicknamed "the black cadet" was killed in a fight. Moreover, the typical Boulonnais scenery with its hedges can be admired in all its pride.

One kilometre westward is the **Grisendal water mill** from 1811, the last preserved and working water mill out of seven which used to be in operation around Wimille. The miller, who worked here until 1982, occasionally sets the machinery in motion for visitors.

Past **Wimille** and the **Lozembrune castle** you see **Napoleon** from a distance on his lonely 53 metre **column**, erected in 1841 in memory of the first distribution of medals of the Légion d'Honneur on 16 August 1804.

The town of **Boulogne-sur-Mer** developed at the mouth of the river Liane. The town has a long and eventful history: Caesar, Napoleon and Caligula too have been here. Countless monuments and Roman relics commemorate the town's history. The old town centre consists of a high, walled rectangle of around 400 by 300 metres, coinciding with the contours of three succeeding walls built between the Roman era and the start of the Middle Ages.

The oldest monument is the 12th century **Belfort**, access to which can be gained via the 18th century **town hall**. In the latter, the wedding room with its beautiful wooden panelling is particularly worth seeing. The **Notre-Dame Basilica** is famous for the crypt with its painted pillars.

The sea centre of **Nausicaa** along the boulevard is well worth a visit. This is a large nature study centre, reinforcing Boulogne's reputation as the largest fishing port in France. There are a number of huge sea aquaria which together hold 1.5 million litres of water, displaying and interpreting marine life and the laws of nature that determine it.

Having finally reached the sea again it is worth exploring the coast, very different from the Dutch coast. Having left behind the low-lying, sandy, dune landscape, we have now reached striking, brilliant white cliffs plunging into the sea. Our international journey has taken us from one landscape to another; in future, the development of European routes will induce us to travel yet further across northern France and onwards to the Iberian peninsula.

sandstone house from 1755. At the end of the 18th century, early 19th century this used to be the home of sisters who cared for the sick and helped raise children from poor families in the area.

The village of Le Wast also features **Sint-Michels church**, which was built between 1086 and 1109 - around the times of the first crusade. It is the last remnant of a monastery which was established in those days by the later canonized Ide, mother of Godfried of Bouillon.

The route continues through the settlements of **Belle-et-Houllefort** and **Conteville-les-Boulogne**, where the typical architecture of the traditional houses is a striking element. Between the latter village and Pernes-les-Boulogne it passes the 16th century brick mansion of **Senlecques** , where tourists can now stay overnight in a room or camp on the grounds.

In the village of **Pernes-les-Boulogne** the route crosses the small river **Wimereux**. The name originates from the Latin Vimen Revus meaning "reed river". Further west the route continues in the river valley where the village of **Pittefaux** is situated. This is where the **Souverain-Moulin castle** was built between 1624 and 1645 on the ruins of its predecessor. An additional storey was then added in the 19th century. With its moats and annexes, among which is a robust dovecote, the castle is a breathtaking sight. Opposite the castle is a pretty little brick **church**.

The route continues through the Wimereux

Accommodation

Hotels and guest houses
59- **Licques**, "La Badoule", Rue de Breuil 427, 21.85.08.29 (chambres d'hôtes)
60- **Licques**, "Legru", Rue de Licques 481, 21.36.22.90 (gîte)
61- **Licques**, Hôtel Chez René", Avenue de Lumbres 316, 21.35.00.31
62- **Belle en Houllefort**, Mme de Montigny, "Le Breucq", 21.83.37.03 (chambres d'hôtes)
63- **Pernes-les-Boulognes**, "Le Petit Fauquehove", 21.83.37.03 (chambres d'hôtes)
64- **Wimille**, "Café-Hôtel de la Colonne", Rue Napoléon 29
65- **Boulogne-sur-Mer**, Boutroy family, Place la Mairie, 21.85.20.19 (chambres d'hôtes)
66- **Boulogne-sur-Mer**, "Hôtel Faidherbe", Rue Faidherbe 12, 21.31.60.93
67- **Boulogne-sur-Mer**, "Hôtel de France", Rue Victor Hugo 83, 21.87.42.00
68- **Boulogne-sur-Mer**, "Hôtel de Londres", Place de France 22, 21.31.35.63
69- **Boulogne-sur-Mer**, "Hôtel de Lorraine", Place de Lorraine 7, 21.31.34.78
70- **Boulogne-sur-Mer**, "Hôtel le Mirador", Rue de la Lampe 2/4, 21.31.38.08
71- **Boulogne-sur-Mer**, "Hôtel le Sleeping", Boulevard Daunou 18, 21.80.62.79
72- **Boulogne-sur-Mer**, "Nouvel Hôtel", Rue Félix Adam, 21.31.39.63

Campsites
54- **Licques**, "Le Canchy", Rue de Canchy, 21.82.63.41
55- **La Capelle-les-Boulogne**, "Camping Municipal les Sapins", 21.83.16.61

Tourist Attractions

Colembert-Le Wast
Maison du Parc Naturel Régional
(information on Boulonnais Natural Park), Manoir de Huisbois, 21.83.38.79

Boulogne-sur-Mer
Nausicaa, National Sea Centre
(information on marine life), Boulevard, 21.30.99.99
Chateau Musee

Tourist Information

Wimereux, Quai Alfred Giard, 21.83.27.17
Boulogne-sur-Mer, Rue Désille 24, 21.83.96.77
Boulogne-sur-Mer, Forum Jean-Noël, 21.31.68.3

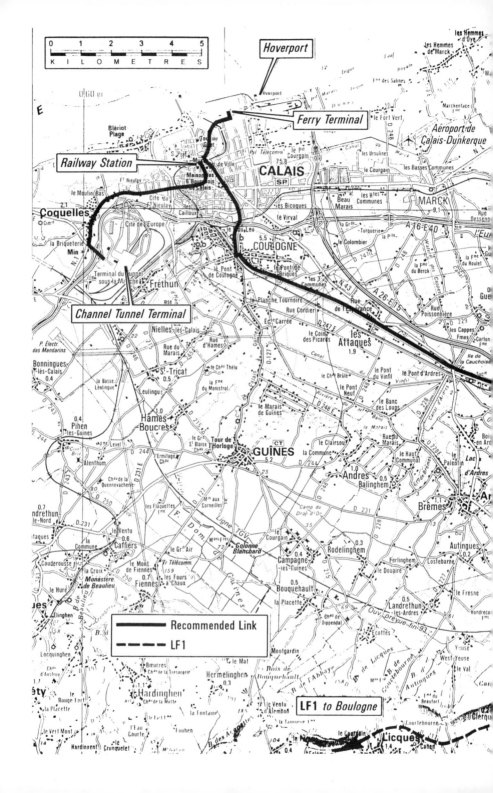

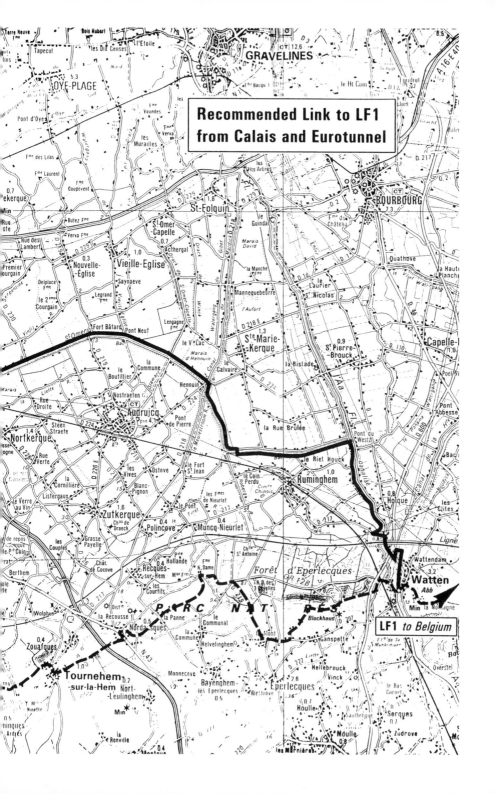

Recommended Link to LF1 from Calais and Eurotunnel

LF1 *to Belgium*

Watten (LF1 route) to Calais

From the centre of Watten take the main street towards St Omer as far as the bridge. Just before the bridge turn right and follow the canal to the lock (1km). Cross the canal - we hope to negotiate signage for this section soon but do take care, as it is easy to go wrong here.

After crossing the canal turn left to rejoin it. After 300m continue to follow the canal as it turns right, where a sign for canal boats indicates Calais. Follow the canal for 1km passing under three bridges. Turn left at the fourth bridge, after 300m turn right and continue for 200m to rejoin the canal. After 2kms on the left is an old chicory drier.

Continue until the canal divides. Turn left and you are now on the Calais-St Omer canal. After approximately 2km cross over the canal by a small bridge and continue along the canal for 5km through the Marais (marshes) to a lock at Hennuin, where you can find some shops. Continue out of Hennuin on the right of the canal for 10km until you pass underneath the motorway. At this point is a large sugar factory - if you visit in October or November you will be impressed by the aroma. At Pont D'Ardres cross the main bridge, don't take D228, N43 but turn left to rejoin the right hand side of the canal and continue for 3km to the village of Les Attaques. Another 7km and you arrive at Coulogne, a suburb of Calais; cross by the iron bridge to the left hand side of the canal. Here too you may be impressed by the aroma; ride as fast as you can past a smelly factory and head underneath the motorway bridge.
You should now be able to see the 75m tower of Calais Town Hall. After about 2km more you arrive in the centre of Calais. At the end of the canal turn left and then after 100m right. Do as local cyclists do, cross by the old railway bridge (Pont Faiderbe). When you arrive at Danemark Square, go straight on to Rue de Bruxelle, straight on again to Rue de Londres and straight on to the bridge (Pont Vetillard). From the other side of the bridge you can follow signs to the Ferry Terminal.

Calais is the City of the famous Six Burghers, who were ready to sacrifice themselves to save their City. It is well equipped with hotels, restaurants and specialist shops, and worth delaying your departure longer than the typical car-borne visitor. Tourist information is at 12, Boulevard Clemenceau, tel 21 36 62 40.

Calais to Eurotunnel

This is very much an interim route. We hope to negotiate much improved cycle access to the Eurotunnel Terminal in the near future.

From Calais Station follow Boulevard Jacquard to Place Albert 1er. Turn right to Boulevard Gambetta as far as a roundabout with cycle lanes. Go straight on to Avenue Salengro and continue for 3km to the village of Coquelles. Pass the church on your right and at the roundabout turn left. At the next roundabout turn left and follow signs to the Tourist Terminal. Bon Voyage!